Traditional Quaker Christianity

Assembled and edited by
Terry H. Wallace
Susan S. Smith
John C. Smith
Arthur Berk

Copyright © 2014 by Ohio Yearly Meeting

Published by Ohio Yearly Meeting
c/o Olney Friends School
61830 Sandy Ridge Road
Barnesville, OH 43713-1176
USA

ISBN: 978-0-9701375-8-6

Available in both paperback and e-book editions

Available through
Amazon.com
BarnesandNoble.com
Foundation Publications
Ohio Yearly Meeting

Cover art work by Matthew Bowman, *chalkevangelist.com*
Cover and Book design by *Publish Wholesale*

TABLE OF CONTENTS

Introduction ix

Chapter 1: JESUS CHRIST: THE BASIS OF QUAKER FAITH
AND PRACTICE 1
   Section 1.A: Jesus Christ Is the Word of God 3
   Section 1.B: God's Old and New Covenants
     with Humanity 8
   Section 1.C: Atonement and Reconciliation
     with Our Creator 12
   Section 1.D: Righteousness, Holiness,
     and the Power of God 15

Chapter 2: THE SCRIPTURES 21
   Section 2.A: Making Use of Scripture 23
   Section 2.B: Are the Scriptures Essential to Salvation? 31
   Section 2.C: Ways of Exploring the Bible 35
   Section 2.D: The Psalms and Other Scripture Passages 38

Chapter 3: THE INWARD LIFE 45
   Section 3.A: The Spiritual Search 47
   Section 3.B: Inward States, Dryness, and the Daily Cross 50
   Section 3.C: The Unchangeable Teacher,
     Prophet, Shepherd 53
   Section 3.D: "I Heard A Voice...." 56
   Section 3.E: Spiritual Baptism 59
   Section 3.F: Spiritual Communion 62
   Section 3.G: Discerning Leadings 65
   Section 3.H: "What Canst Thou Say?" 68
   Section 3.I: "Be Still and Cool...." 71
   Section 3.J: Knowing Christ in Us 75

Chapter 4: WAITING WORSHIP 79

Chapter 5: MINISTRY AND MINISTERS 89
   Section 5.A: The Call to Ministry 91
   Section 5.B: Women Ministers 96
   Section 5.C: Speaking during Worship 99
   Section 5.D: Advice to Ministers 104
   Section 5.E: The Traveling Ministry
      and Visiting Families 107
   Section 5.F: Examples of the Nature of Ministry from
      Quaker History 113
      Example 1: James Scribbens 113
      Example 2: Isaac Lawton and A Servant Boy 116

Chapter 6: CHRIST'S PEOPLE: THE CHURCH VISIBLE
   AND INVISIBLE 119
   Section 6.A: Christ's People 121
   Section 6.B: The Church Visible and Invisible 123
   Section 6.C: The Place of the Individual
      in the Body of Christ 129
   Section 6.D: Clerking: An Aid for Decision-Making 133
   Section 6.E: The Advices and Queries 140
   Section 6.F: Spirit-Led Teachers 145
   Section 6.G: Eldering and Oversight 147

Chapter 7: FAITHFUL LIVING 157
   Section 7.A: Our Lives as Our Testimony 159
   Section 7.B: The Lamb's War 161
   Section 7.C: The Lamb's War and Peace 165
   Section 7.D: The Peace Testimony:
      Common Misunderstandings 168
   Section 7.E: Friends' Original Peace Witness 173
   Section 7.F: Simplicity and Plainness 179
   Section 7.G: Integrity 182
   Section 7.H: An Example of Faithful Living—
      John Woolman 185
   Section 7.I: Our Lamb's War Today 188

APPENDICES 195
    Appendix 1: Eldering and Oversight Readings 197
    Appendix 2: A Brief Glossary to Quaker Terminology 201
    Appendix 3: Modern Quakerism, A Fragmented Society 210
    Appendix 4: A Bibliography for Further Reading 217

JESUS CHRIST IN THE MIDST OF HIS PEOPLE

When Christ is present in the midst of His gathered people, the type of worship, of business procedure, and of action is radically changed from Old Testament times.

As people gather for worship, they have Christ present to be their High Priest. He directs the worship and the ministry of the group. No one orders a program of worship and no one is responsible for a prearranged message, as all is done under the immediate guidance of God, Christ, and the Holy Spirit. This is the worship that belongs to the new covenant and is worship in Spirit and in Truth.

The business of the Church is carried on under the lordship of Christ. The people of God meet together to learn the mind of Christ on the business before them. If even one person is not clear as to what should be done, it is a serious matter. Since all go to the same Source—Christ—all should agree on the guidance. Where there is not agreement, all should wait in a spirit of worship and prayer until they can move ahead as a united group doing the will of God.

The early Friends held that there were certain actions that God requires of us under the new covenant. One of the most pertinent for our day is the peace testimony. They believed that the Lord had redeemed them from the occasion of war. Christ by His living Presence had freed them from war. As a witness or testimony, they were to refrain from it. And, through the power of Christ, they were to live lives of honesty, simplicity, and freedom from racial or other forms of prejudice.

The people of God are the Church of Christ. Under Him, the individual has freedom without anarchy, and the group is united in worship, work, and witness without becoming a dictatorship over the individual. Fallible human beings are brought to know the will of God who is perfect. Those who are not a people are brought to be a people.

These people die, yet they know eternal life. They suffer, yet they rejoice. They are weak and frail, yet they are made more than conquerors. All this and more the people of God have through Jesus Christ.

-John H. Curtis, *A Quaker View of the Christian Revelation*

INTRODUCTION

Traditional Quaker Christianity is the work of many hands. The first very rough draft was developed by Michael Hatfield, who generated it in his own study of Friends' faith and witness. Many of us who saw his early draft thought it could be of great value to inquirers, new members, and old hands alike. Michael gifted his manuscript to Ohio Yearly Meeting to do with as it saw fit, recognizing it was both in its first very rough draft and as yet untested as a study guide. Other Friends in the yearly meeting subsequently utilized it in small group discussions and found it quite helpful, though the discussions also pointed up numerous areas needing further clarification, development, and even occasional correction.

In 2012, OYM's Representative Meeting appointed an editing committee to bring *Traditional Quaker Christianity* to publishable form. Members of the committee included Arthur Berk, John and Susan Smith, and Terry Wallace, its work being monitored for Representative Meeting by Conrad Lindes. In the ensuing eighteen months, the editing committee made extensive changes to the original draft, including a complete reorganization of the original text from fifty-two discussions on discrete topics to the present chapter and section organization on key subjects:

    Jesus Christ, the Basis of Quaker Faith and Practice
    The Scriptures
    The Inward Life
    Waiting Worship
    Ministry and Ministers
    Christ's People
    Faithful Living

The editorial committee attached four appendices: 1) "Further Readings on Eldership and Eldering," 2) "A Glossary to Quaker Terminology," and 3) "Modern Quakerism: A Fragmented Society."

The third appendix will help inquirers begin to differentiate our faith and practice from those of a number of other bodies bearing the name of "Quaker." Finally, the committee attached 4) a bibliography citing good sources for further reading and exploration.

Chapter 1
JESUS CHRIST: THE BASIS OF QUAKER FAITH AND PRACTICE

Section 1.A
Jesus Christ Is the Word of God

Readings: *The Word of God is Jesus Christ* by T.H.S. Wallace; *Friends' Understanding of the Word of God* by Jack Smith

The belief that Jesus Christ is the Word of God is the foundation upon which all vital Friends' practices stand.

What the Bible says about the Word of God: The Bible is clear that Christ is the Word. The Gospel of John, in its profound first chapter, is straightforward:

> In the beginning was the Word, and the Word was with God, and the Word was God. He was with God in the beginning. Through him all things were made; without him nothing was made that has been made. In him was life, and that life was the light of men (John 1:1-4).

John clearly refers to Christ Jesus in this passage. The Revelation of John is no less definite, envisioning the triumphant Christ leading the armies of heaven forward to the Last Judgment:

> I saw heaven standing open and there before me was a white horse, whose rider is called Faithful and True. With justice he judges and makes war. His eyes are like blazing fire, and on his head are many crowns. He has a name written on him that no one knows but he himself. He is dressed in a robe dipped in blood, and his name is the Word of God. The armies of heaven were following him, riding on white horses dressed in fine linen, white and clean. Out of his mouth comes a sharp sword with which to strike down the nations... (Rev.19:11-15).

The unusual change in John's description from past tense to present above is neither a translation error nor an exotic claim. John stresses that Christ Jesus is powerfully present and speaking now. His words are striking the nations. People are feeling His presence as He cuts to evil, exposes it, and destroys it.

Not only is Jesus the Word of God, but, as the Word, He continues to be present among and speak with people who will listen. Jesus Himself asserted His continuing presence in the world—even after His ascension. Jesus' promise of "the Counselor" in John 14 emphatically declares the mystery that all three—Father, Son, Holy Spirit—will be present in us:

> And I will ask the Father, and he will give you another Counselor to be with you forever- the Spirit of Truth. The world cannot accept him, because it neither sees him nor knows him. But you know him, for he lives with you and will be in you. I will not leave you as orphans; I will come to you. Before long, the world will not see me anymore, but you will see me. Because I live, you also will live. On that day you will realize that I am in my Father, and you are in me, and I am in you. Whoever has my commands and obeys them, he is the one who loves me. He who loves me will be loved by my Father, and I too will love him and show myself to him (John 14:16-21).

When Jesus said, "I will not leave you orphaned," he was referring to the loss the disciples would feel when he died. He promised to return "in a little while" and reveal himself to them. Jesus clearly will continue to love and manifest himself to those who love him and keep his commandments. Jesus also appeared at work in the world after the ascension, when he temporarily blinded Saul on the Damascus road. Saul asks, "Who are you, Lord?" And Christ answers, "I am Jesus whom you are persecuting."

Finally, Jesus firmly rebuked those who depended on scripture alone for their salvation. They are in danger of missing, not hearing, and not being taught by the real Word of God. He tells the Jews of Jerusalem: "You search the Scriptures because you think that in them you have eternal life; and it is they that testify on my behalf; yet you refuse to come to me to have life" (John 5:39-40).

Jesus is the One who gives us a right understanding of the Scriptures. The Scriptures declare that Jesus is our present Teacher, the one who opens the mysteries of the Bible (1 John 2:27). Jesus can make clear the meaning of the Scriptures because He embodies the Spirit of God, through Whom the Bible was given to humanity. One of the primary works of Jesus, after the resurrection, is opening Scripture to His disciples, both on the Emmaus Road (Luke 24:13+) and in Jerusalem (Luke 24:36+). Furthermore, Peter's antidote to the poison of "the ignorant and unstable" who "twist [Paul's writings] to their own destruction ... as they do other scriptures" is not more Scripture. His recommendation is simple, yet profound: "Grow in the grace and knowledge of our Lord and Savior Jesus Christ" (2 Peter 3:14-18). Indeed, without Jesus who opens and interprets Scripture today, just as He did for the disciples, we will be lost in the staggering Babel of the world's and the churches' conflicting and confusing interpretations.

George Fox's experience of Who the Word Is. One of many people who discovered the Word of God through the right use of the Bible was George Fox. He came of age in the 1640s when religious ferment and confusion were turning England inside out—politically, socially, economically, and spiritually. He searched the Scriptures for answers to his questions, especially his temptation to despair of salvation. Beyond consulting the Bible, he sought out the chief priests and preachers "to look for comfort but found no comfort from them" (*The Journal of George Fox*, Nickall's edition, p.4). Worldly men, they prescribed only worldly interventions, all sorts of seventeenth-century medicinal and psychological treatments, from bleeding and purging, to tobacco (to calm the nerves) and psalm singing (music to sooth the savage breast). Fox found no real, no living knowledge of Jesus Christ among the Christians of his day. For him, they were people "holding to the outward form of godliness but denying its power" (2 Tim. 3:5).

Fox recognized that the Bible was an important starting point and essential source book for beginning to understand the ways of God with men and women. He studied carefully the lives of Jesus and the ancient men and women of God, as set forth in the Scriptures. He realized that they walked by the Lord's direct revelation of His will and showed forth His power in their obedience and their deeds. However, when Fox compared their words and deeds with the doctrines of religious leaders of his own day, he saw that the latter had clearly diverged from the former.

Yet, the Bible was more than a source book for Fox. It was his check on spiritual development. As he experienced spiritual revelations, he found that his "openings" "answered one another and answered the Scriptures..." (Fox, *Journal*, p.7-8). As God revealed truth to Fox, he found that each new revelation agreed with others he had experienced and that each corresponded specifically to understandings he had gained through the Scriptures.

Those two checks are of exceptional importance in the search for spiritual truth. God's continuing revelation of Himself is not a series of discrete events, each exposing a new truth, each new truth perhaps in conflict or contradiction to past revelations. Rather, God's continuing revelation is unified. Present-day revelation confirms and answers that of the past. Fox recognized that Christ Jesus, by Whom he was guided, is the same yesterday, today, and tomorrow (Hebrews 13:8). Christ is not changeable so as to reveal something as evil at one point and later move us toward it as good. Thus, the consistency of present with past revelation is a check against that all too human tendency to devise clever rationalizations, to twist what we have received to suit our own purposes and desires.

DISCUSSION QUESTIONS:

1. There are millions of people in the world who claim a "personal relationship with Jesus Christ," and there are many possible meanings for that phrase. How did Fox understand his relationship with Jesus Christ?
2. Does the traditional Quaker understanding of the Word of God surprise you? How so?
3. Experience tends to be valued because it seems undeniable. Yet, over time, we often come to deeper or different understandings of prior experiences. How do you evaluate your personal experiences?

Section 1.B
God's Old and New Covenants with Humanity

Readings: Jeremiah 31:31-34; John 1:1-9; Acts 2:14-21; Hebrews 8; Robert Barclay, APOLOGY FOR THE TRUE CHRISTIAN DIVINITY Prop. 10, §§ 1-3; Prop. 11, § XIV; Prop. 14, § 3; Prop. 15, § 15; Lewis Benson, "George Fox's Conception of the Church," "The Universal Dimension in the Thought of George Fox," and "The Universal Message of George Fox" in THE QUAKER VISION; John H. Curtis, *A Quaker View of the Christian Revelation* (Tract Association of Friends).

Outward gatherings and godly individuals. In the Christian understanding, there have been two outward gatherings of God's people. The first gathering was that of the Old Covenant, while the second is that of the New Covenant.

These covenants express an intentional relationship between God and groups of people, not merely individuals. Throughout the Old Testament, there are stories of individuals who were obedient to God's Spirit but who were not part of God's Old Covenant people. God's physical gathering of a people does not deny God's activity in the lives of individuals outside the group. Rather, it illustrates that what God intends to convey to humanity is a message and a Spirit too great to be contained within individual lives. God's message requires the shared life of a gathered people. A gathered people can show forth more divine power than a collection of individuals, and being part of a gathered people provides clarity, power, and community to the individual.

The Old Covenant. Under the Old Covenant, God gathered people as a religious nation. There were religious rites and ceremonies, and there were governmental laws and regulations. There were kings, judges, and priests. There was an army.

This religious nation carried the message that there was one God. This religious nation carried the message that God required justice. This religious nation carried many messages Christians continue to this day. But this religious nation was limited in the messages it could carry. It was limited by its being a nation. Nations make war. Nations defend territory. Nations include criminals and innocents. Nations police and punish.

The New Covenant. Before the life of Jesus, God's Spirit was at work in individual lives, but under the New Covenant, Jesus makes possible a greater outpouring of the Holy Spirit. This greater gift of the Spirit marks a difference in degree of relationship with God. It is the same gift, but more of it. It is the same Spirit, but more of it. The New Covenant is the gathering of God's people directly by God's Spirit. In presenting the New Covenant, God offers to His church the same relationship He offers to individuals: to be led by His Spirit, to be the temple of His Spirit, to be His visible body. The New Covenant focuses on the spiritual life of a gathered people rather than on individualized spirituality. The New Covenant is open to everyone who accepts it.

Believing Jesus to be the Messiah, Christians understand the New Covenant to be a more complete revelation of God's will than the Old Covenant. Friends have referred to specific scriptural descriptions of the New Covenant in highlighting our understanding of it.

The eighth chapter of Hebrews, where the New Covenant is described, reviews God's promises (in Jeremiah 31:31-34) to forgive the sins of His people, to write His laws directly upon their minds and hearts, and to be so intimately known by each of His people that there is no need for His people to teach one another—all of God's people will know Him directly and personally. Friends emphasize being taught by God directly and personally. We are all to know God. This knowledge is Eternal Life (John 17:3).

In Acts 2, the New Covenant is portrayed as the outpouring of God's Spirit upon all of humanity. It is promised that all God's servants, both men and women, shall "prophesy"—that is, shall outwardly reveal messages that have been inwardly received from the Holy Spirit. Friends' worship and witness to others are understood as prophecy, in the sense of obeying God's Voice within us in order to manifest God's will to others.[1] Friends expect both men and women to participate in vocal ministry during worship, to be active in explaining our faith and practices to others, and to live lives that exemplify our beliefs.

In addition to a "gender-neutral" expectation for the expression of our faith ("in Christ there is neither male nor female" Gal.3:28), another implication of the Spirit being poured onto everyone is that we have a connection with everyone we meet. Christ's promptings are within each human being. Friends often refer to this connection as the Light of Christ that "enlightens everyone" (John 1:9).

The Light of Christ reveals to us our darkness—our sinful attitudes and actions that block the Light. But the Light also reveals how we can be saved from these sins, which is to follow Christ's promptings within us—to call upon and follow Christ as Lord. The journals and other writings of Friends express both the pain of recognizing the darkness within them and the clarity of recognizing the Light as they were obedient to Christ's leading.

The New Covenant also introduces changes in the manner of worship. Jesus declares in John 4:23-24, "Yet a time is coming and has now come when the true worshipers will worship the Father in spirit and truth, for they are the kind of worshipers the Father seeks. God is spirit, and his worshipers must worship in spirit and

---

[1] Prophecy rarely involves foretelling future events, even though in today's popular usage foretelling is emphasized to the exclusion of other kinds of prophetic speaking. Friends have always considered vocal ministry during worship to be a key aspect of New Covenant prophecy. On only limited occasions such as the vision of Joseph Hoag (described below), Friends believed themselves to be foretelling future events.

in truth" (John 4:23-24). No outward ceremonies or rites are required for the worshiper to be accepted in God's Presence. Instead, faithful people are to practice fairness, loving kindness, and humbly doing what God directs (Micah 6:6-8).

Finally, the group of people gathered into the New Covenant is not a nation but the Church, the body of people drawn together in following Christ. The people of the New Covenant do not engage in physical violence characteristic of warring nations, but they are willing to use love, faith, and hope against forces of evil and darkness. (1 Thessalonians 5:8; 2 Corinthians 10:3-5; John 18:36; Matthew 26:52-53)

DISCUSSION QUESTIONS:

1. The "Old Covenant" and "New Covenant" are scriptural concepts that were commonly known in early Friends' times, and commonly used by early Friends. What about those concepts do you find useful?
2. Whereas the Old Covenant involved a nation-state, the New Covenant involves the Church. What implications does this have for our understanding of our relationship to the state?
3. Being spiritually connected with others through Christ is the basis of true sharing among us—and an essential element of the New Covenant. How can we distinguish sharing based on our connection through Christ from sharing based on common backgrounds, interests, situations, or emotional needs?
4. What is it to know God directly? How do we discern who truly knows God? How do we know if we do? How can we distinguish the Spirit's leading and voice from our personal impulses, preferences, and thoughts—or the leading and voice of other spirits?
5. What other implications of the New Covenant impress you especially?

Section 1.C
Atonement and Reconciliation with Our Creator

Readings: Matthew 13; Luke 13:34-35, 19:41-44; John 1:9, 3:16, 6:53-57, 15; Romans 1:16-32, 8; 1 Corinthians 6:15-19, 12; Galatians 3:27; Colossians 1:21-23; Hebrews 6:4-6; 2 Peter 2:15-22, 3:9; 1 John 1:5-10, 2:15-17; Robert Barclay, APOLOGY FOR THE TRUE CHRISTIAN DIVINITY Prop. 5-8 (Freiday).

Salvation through Obedience. Barclay sets forth Friends' traditional understanding of an individual's reconciliation with God:

> First, God, who out of his infinite love sent his Son the Lord Jesus Christ into the world, and who tasted death for everyone, has given a certain day or time of visitation to everyone, whether Jew or Gentile ... or of whatever nation.... During that day or time of visitation, it is possible for them to saved ....
>
> Secondly, for this purpose God has communicated, and given a measure of the light of his own Son, a measure of grace, or a measure of the Spirit to every man....
>
> Thirdly, God, in and by this light and seed, invites, calls, exhorts, and strives with every man, in order to save him. If this light is received and not resisted, it works the salvation of all, even those who are ignorant of the death and sufferings of Christ.... It does this not only by bringing them a sense of their own misery, but by allowing them to share inwardly in the sufferings of Christ. They participate in his resurrection by becoming holy, pure, and righteous, and by recovering from their sins [Freiday, pp. 82-83].

Salvation, as understood by Friends, is premised upon Jesus having "tasted death for everyone," but it is distinctive in several ways. First, Jesus who tasted death for everyone enlightens everyone—literally everyone, even those who have never heard the story of Jesus. The story of Jesus (what Barclay calls "the history") profits, comforts, and encourages those who know it, but even those who have never heard it can be enlightened by the Holy Spirit of Jesus. This is the "gospel preached to every creature" (Mark 16:15) and the Light given to everyone. It is Christ within us—even before we recognize Him.

Second, an individual is saved by following the Light of Christ, which is the means of participating in the resurrection of Christ and becoming holy like Jesus. It is actual obedience to the Light of Christ, rather than intellectual beliefs or rituals, that transmits the saving power of God. Since one is redeemed through obedience, so long as an individual is faithful to what has been personally required, he or she is redeemed. What God requires differs—what was required of Mary or Paul—was more than what is required of most of us. How much is required depends upon how much one is given. But there is no reconciliation that is separate from actual obedience and right-living.

Third, the time in which the Holy Spirit is actively pleading within us is limited. The time occurs differently for each of us. But, when it occurs, it must be accepted. Resisting the Holy Spirit leads us to have a hardened and unresponsive heart. Thankfully, we are assured, the Lord is patient, desiring that we all be saved. He even converted the persecuting Saul to become the apostle Paul.

DISCUSSION QUESTIONS:

1. Friends' understanding of the at-one-ment is that the saving Light within each of us is the Spirit of Christ made accessible to us through the obedient life and death of Jesus. How does this resonate within you?

2. Barclay says that God's Light is not part of "human nature" but part of the nature of Jesus Christ. By our obedience to the Light, we participate in the nature of Jesus Christ. Early Friends understood following the Light as difficult, as bearing the cross, as having our personal nature spiritually crucified in order to be spiritually resurrected. In what ways is following the Light hard, and in what ways is it easy? How do we know when the "hard parts" are of our own making rather than Christ's? What about the "easy parts?"
3. Early Friends understood obedience as essential to reconciliation. What is required of each individual differs. This is relative in that it is personalized according to the measure of the Holy Spirit given, but it is universal in that it requires obedience of everyone. What does it mean that different measures of the Light are given to different individuals?
4. What do you make of the "day of visitation" and the risk of our hearts hardening? Have you experienced one—or both? Can we know if another person's day has already gone —or come?
5. What is resonating most deeply within you?

Section 1.D
Righteousness, Holiness, and the Power of God

Readings: Thomas Evans, "A Concise Account of the Religious Society of Friends, Commonly Called Quakers" (Tract Association of Friends); Lewis Benson, *Catholic Quakerism* (republished in the United Kingdom as *A Universal Christian Faith*).

Lewis Benson, in his *Catholic Quakerism*, examines George Fox's understanding of God's call to righteousness. Benson begins by contrasting two "Christian ethics," or ways of looking at what is expected of a Christian.

> The ethic of idealism starts with ideal social ends or goals, and it sees religion as a force leading to the realization of these goals. The Christian idealist sees morality as the struggle to attain moral goals, and he finds a ... gap between the ultimate moral good and the Christian's present ability to live up to it. This approach takes for granted that there can be an unresolvable tension between what a Christian knows he ought to do and what, in fact, he is able to do. (pp. 23-24)
>
> The ethic of obligation, on the other hand, sees right action as a response to God's command. It begins with the assertion, "He hath showed thee, O man, what is good...." (p. 24)
>
> Fox's Christian ethic is an ethic of obligation, not an ethic of idealism. The call to righteousness is a call to do something or to refrain from doing something, and that which the eternal voice commands is never beyond our power to obey.... This leaves no room for the plea, "I know what God wants me to do but I haven't the power to do it." The choice is between obedience and disobedience.... Penington says, "As the soul in

faith gives itself up to obey, so the power appears and works the obedience.... The power never fails the faith." (Penington, *Works* (1761) I, 556.).... This belief that Christ teaches us the principles of God's righteousness and gives us the power to obey them is the greatest single factor in the formation of "the Quaker character".... Fox says, "This way of holiness that the prophets prophesied of is Christ Jesus, the way," and he observes that the call of God is that "all may walk in holiness as becomes the house of God." (pp. 25-30)

The apostle Peter advised Christians to be "holy in all your conduct" (1 Peter 1:15-16), referring to an Old Testament command from God, "Be holy, for I am holy" (Leviticus 11:44). To be holy is to be fully obedient to God, to live in God's righteousness through His power. When we are holy, we have consecrated ourselves, and all we are and do, to the purposes of God. We live each day guided by God, not by the values and ways of the world. We live according to our Lord's teaching and direction.

Self-denying and deeply engaged. Thomas Evans, a nineteenth century Philadelphia Friend, described early Friends, emphasizing their holiness and obedience to God:

> A distinguishing trait in the character of the primitive Friends was the earnestness with which they enforced, both by example and precept, the indispensable obligation of a life of holiness in the fear of God. While they felt the necessity of having a sound and firm belief in all the doctrines of the Christian religion as set forth in the Holy Scriptures, they were also convinced that unless this belief was carried out in the daily walk and conversation, and accompanied by those fruits of the Spirit that are the evidences of true faith, as well as the ornament of the Christian, it would be of little avail.

Recognizing in its full extent the declaration, "Except a man be born again, he cannot see the kingdom of God," (John 3:3) and the test laid down by the Saviour of men, "By their fruits shall ye know them", as well as his solemn words, "Not everyone that saith unto me, Lord, Lord, shall enter into the kingdom of heaven, but he that doeth the will of my Father which is in heaven" (Matthew 7:20, 21), they were concerned to warn all against the delusive notion that men might live in sin and in the indulgence of their carnal wills and appetites, and yet be saved by a professed dependence on what the Lord Jesus Christ has graciously done in his flesh for the redemption of mankind.

They were plain, practical, self-denying men and women, deeply and earnestly engaged to walk in the obedience of faith to all the requirements of the Divine law; and their minds being enlightened from on high to see the true spiritual nature and the transforming effects of the religion of the gospel, they apprehended that many of its professors were resting their hopes of salvation on a mere assent of the understanding to the truths recorded in the Holy Scriptures, and in the compliance with outward ceremonies, without bringing forth those "good works which were before ordained that we should walk in them." The inward life of righteousness in the daily fear of God being the great object of their earnest concern and engagement, both for themselves and others, they called on their hearers to come home into their own hearts and examine, in the light that Christ gives, whether they were clean and pure, or defiled and unholy.

With no less earnestness, they pressed upon all the necessity of a close attention and obedience to the teachings of the Spirit of Truth in the heart, as the great enlightener and sanctifier of man and his guide in things pertaining to salvation; as the true light by which every one might come to see his own state, as seen by the Searcher of hearts, and be shown the way to come out of the thralldom of sin into the glorious liberty of the children of God.

They invited men to come to and believe in Christ Jesus the Lord, not only as testified of in the Bible as the Redeemer, Propitiation, Mediator and Intercessor with the Father for lost fallen man, but also as he reveals himself in the heart by his Spirit as the true Light; showing man his undone condition in the fall, and the means by which he may be brought out of it by being born again of the Spirit; and also as a swift witness against evil, and a comforter for well doing. Esteeming this knowledge as the very essence of true religion, they dwelt much upon it in their ministry and writings, and even in their dying sayings enjoined it on their hearers, as of the first importance to all who hoped for salvation.

DISCUSSION QUESTIONS:

1. Why does the Quaker ethic of obligation make far more sense than an ethic of idealism? What are the dangers of trying to pursue an ethic of idealism?
2. What do you make of Thomas Evans's description of the first Friends, who lived two centuries before him? What evidence do you think he used?
3. Do you agree that a life of holiness is an "indispensable obligation" for those who seek to follow Christ Jesus? In answering this question, what are you considering "life of holiness" to mean?
4. Living totally according to God's teaching and direction sounds like a major undertaking. In this section, Benson echoes Penington's assertion that God gives sufficient grace for everything He requires of us. What help does God offer you to

live in holiness? Do you find that God's help is sometimes more available than at other times? Explain.
5. What is resonating most deeply within you?

Chapter 2
THE SCRIPTURES

Section 2.A
Making Use of Scripture

Readings: *2 Timothy 3:16;* George Fox, *The Journal of George Fox,* Nickall's edition, Chapters 1 and 2.

Our heritage as Friends connects us with the Bible. The first Friends found that the Scriptures, the name Friends have traditionally used for the Bible[2], confirmed the faith they experienced, and they drew extensively upon the Scriptures to communicate their own convictions. For many Friends today, the Bible continues to be a source of instruction, inspiration, and words with which to give their own testimony. The Scriptures present a record of the timeless complexities of the human interaction with God, while their spiritual quality opens opportunities for deeper prayer and fuller awareness of God's purposes. We can make use of what has been recorded in the Scriptures, bringing ourselves closer to a spiritually satisfying relationship with God.

Scripture is illuminated by the true Word of God. The Scriptures are one way through which God has made His truth available to men and women. However, the Bible gives nothing spiritually special to the reader or the hearer who is not touched by the Spirit of God while considering its words. Human beings need the Word of God, Christ who speaks within us, to comprehend the spiritual truths portrayed in the Bible. George Fox sums up how God's power affects our understanding of the Scriptures: "As man comes through by the Spirit and power of God to Christ ... and is led by the Holy Ghost into the truth and substance of the Scriptures, sitting down in him who is the author

---

[2] In fact, that book refers to itself as "scriptures" and nowhere mentions "Bible."

and end of them, then are they read and understood with profit and great delight" (*Journal,* p. 32).

When we allow Christ, the Word of God, to illuminate what we read in the Scriptures, we often find them immediately relevant to our own situation. Reading a Scripture passage can be comforting, inspiring, or sometimes very revealing when the words bring home to us our own shortcomings. As a passage in the Bible itself says, "All Scripture is God-breathed and is useful for teaching, rebuking, correcting and training in righteousness..." (2 Timothy 3:16).

Parallel tracks: religious history and personal spiritual growth. The Bible can be a personal teaching tool, illustrating, correcting, and nurturing our inward spiritual life. At the same time, the Scriptures trace Judeo-Christian religious history. The grand panorama of salvation history from Adam to Christ parallels personal spiritual development.

In the first part of the Old Testament, the Adam to Moses stage, we see both what happened to the Israelites when they turned away from God, and the blessings that followed when they returned to God's ways. Likewise, coming under God's law is a necessary early step in our personal spiritual birth. Without a sense of right or wrong, of what God would and would not have us do, we are creatures of chaos. The biblical chapters detailing the law provide a frame of reference by which we can measure our conduct. We need to know what we must do to be right with God, and to acknowledge our own powerlessness to accomplish that by ourselves. In reading about Adam, Eve, Miriam, Moses, Abraham, Sarah, and the many others through the time of Moses and the wandering Israelites, we can often see ourselves and our present-day religious communities. We can use the Old Testament lessons to detect what is hindering our relationship with God, and to acknowledge our own failures. The confession of failure, brokenness, poverty and helplessness is the point at which we are truly open to the power of God. It is the moment of hope! If we allow ourselves to be convicted, to feel the condemnation of our disobedience, our sin, God will move us forward to the second stage of salvation. We begin to realize that we can seek God's help in overcoming our failures.

After chronicling the wandering Israelites and their eventual settlement in the Promised Land, the Scriptures continue their historical narrative with an account of the "Prophets" – Isaiah, Jeremiah, Micah, and many others. The prophets' words and actions witness to God's active presence in the world; they call us to become God's people walking in His right and wise way. George Fox well defines the internal experience that characterizes this second stage of Judeo-Christian history and of personal spiritual development, when he states: "All must first know the voice crying in the wilderness[3], in their own hearts, which through transgression were become as a wilderness" (*Journal*, p. 32). However, to know that voice in the wilderness, we must begin living in the same divine Spirit that John the Baptist (whose prophetic voice cried in the wilderness) was in and heed the "burning, shining light, which is sent from God" (Fox's *Journal*, p. 32). It is that Spirit which will prepare the way of the Lord in us by making our crooked ways straight and our rough ways smooth. "And all mankind will see God's salvation" (Luke 3:4-6).

The "Prophets" section of the Old Testament is outspoken in its condemnation of transgression, but it also foreshadows the message of love and hope through Christ found in the New Testament. Isaiah and the other prophets, including John the Baptist whose story is actually found in the New Testament, had been taught only the Jewish law and the writings of earlier prophets, but God gave them words to point us to Christ. Jesus Himself declared continuity

---

[3] Fox's writings are full of scriptural references. The "voice crying in the wilderness" and "prepare the way of the Lord" at the end of this paragraph refer to Isaiah 40:3, part of the Scripture later used by Handel as text in his oratorio *Messiah*.

from the law through the prophets to His own work when He said, "Think not that I have come to abolish the law and the prophets. I have come not to abolish them but to fulfill them" (Matthew 5:17). Not only will He not change the law, He condemns anyone who "breaks one of the least of these commandments" or teaches others to do so.

Then Jesus goes one important step further. In the Sermon on the Mount (Matthew 5, 6, and 7), He moves our attention from external observation of the law (for which the Pharisees of His time were famous) to its *internalization.* The law, for instance, tells us we must not kill, but Christ moves inside to the root of killing and tells us our very anger is up for judgment. God cares about both our inward selves and our outward actions.

The New Testament not only provides an expansion of the activities for which we are accountable to God. It also sets forth a new conception of our relationship to God, as it tells of One like unto Moses but greater than Moses, "for the law was given by Moses, but grace and truth came by Jesus Christ." (John 1:17) The New Testament urges us into closer obedience to God ("Not my will, but Thine be done." Luke 22:42) and at the same time promises us the riches of God's peace, joy, and love if we follow Christ's commandments.

The Quaker faith is biblically based. There is no doubt that George Fox and the other first-generation Friends were immersed in the Scriptures, so much so that they knew large portions of it by memory and drew regularly on the Scriptures for both guidance and preaching. Wilmer Cooper writes that George Fox "and other Friends were not only familiar with the Bible, but took it seriously as a religious guide for their lives." *(A Living Faith,* p. 20) As T. Canby Jones notes in his introduction to Fox's pastoral letters, "George Fox knew the Bible so well the vast majority of things he expressed were in the language and style of Scriptures.... The number of allusions to Scripture and the paraphrases of it [in Fox's writings] is enormous." *(The Power of the Lord Is Over All,* p. iv) According to Dean Freiday, early Friends expected those allusions "to have a mnemonic effect, and not only to bring to mind the full text [of the Scripture passage] but to bring a whole range of associations into the consciousness of [their] hearers." *(Nothing without Christ,* p. 66) George Keith, a seventeenth-century associate of Robert Barclay's, wrote: "We have a twofold evidence, which no heretic can justly lay claim to. The one is the inward evidence of the Spirit of God.... The other is the Testimony of the Scriptures, which I affirm in the name of the people called Quakers, is the best external and outward evidence and rule that can be given." (in R. Barclay *Works,* p. 576, quoted in Freiday, p. 68) Early Friends were familiar with the Bible and used it extensively.

The Scriptures offer historical and personal relevance today. The Bible records centuries of God's work with people, including the responses of countless men and women to each other and to the prompting of God. Some Biblical history, like some secular history, involves wars and other atrocities that we would prefer not to claim and which we desire not to repeat. However, our moral objection to those events does not negate their occurrence, nor does it relieve us of the obligation to acknowledge that thread in the tapestry of our religious background. This illustrates Christ's work in coming to transform the faith into one based on love.

In addition to tracing a connection to our religious heritage, the Scriptures offer many examples of individual people reacting with various emotions in interpersonal situations with which we can identify. Joseph's brothers were jealous of their father's attention to him; they plotted to get rid of Joseph. (Genesis 37) David looked with sexual desire at the attractive wife of another man (2 Samuel 11). Zacchaeus was curious about the man (Jesus) attracting a lot of attention in town (Luke 19: 2-7). The good Samaritan reacted with loving care for an injured stranger (Luke 10: 29-37).

In each of these cases, and in many other stories, the Bible suggests a lesson about what happens when people act on their feelings in certain ways. Although the progression of history makes the details of some biblical settings unfamiliar to many Friends, human similarities prevail enough for most of us to apply these lessons to ourselves today. Letting jealousy or sexual desire be our primary motivation is likely to get us into trouble. Acting on curiosity can lead to unexpected experiences. Loving the unloved may not bring immediate reward and may even cost us something, but we uphold loving care as commendable.

The Scriptures also present episodes in which people reacted to an impersonal situation or to a leading from God. A woman was joyful when she found something special she had thought lost (Luke 15: 8-9). Another woman was hopeful that touching Jesus' clothes would stop her bleeding (Matthew 9: 20-22). Peter leaned on intellectual analysis to refute a leading from God (Acts 10:6-16). Ananias questioned God briefly, but he soon found trust and went where he had been sent (Acts 9: 10-18). We can relate to these episodes with hope and joy. Identifying with Peter and Ananias can help us be obedient to the leadings we are given. By exploring these incidents and many others in the Bible, we can find pieces of truth that connect to our own experience and encourage us to walk more closely with God.

The first chapter of this book explains that the Scriptures provide a check for what appears to be a leading from God and a way of testing conflicting religious views. Robert Barclay elaborates in his *Apology*:

> Since [the Scriptures] are universally regarded as written by the dictates of the Holy Spirit, and the errors which have crept in are not bad enough to obscure their clear testimony to the essentials of the Christian faith, we consider them the only proper outward judge of controversies among Christians. Whatever doctrine is contrary to their testimony

may properly be rejected as false.... The motions of the Spirit can never contradict one another, although they sometimes appear to do so in the blind eyes of the natural [person], just as Paul and James, at first, seem to contradict one another (pp. 58-60).

The Bible's spiritual value. Barclay also saw the Scriptures as a useful spiritual mirror:

> In the Scriptures, God has deemed it proper to give us a looking glass by which we can see the conditions and experiences of ancient believers. There we find that our experience is analogous to theirs. We may thus become more confirmed and comforted and strengthened in our hope of obtaining the same end....
>
> This is the great work of the Scriptures, and their usefulness to us. They find a respondent spark in us, and in that way we discern the stamp of God's ways and His Spirit upon them. We know this from the inward acquaintance we have with the same Spirit and with His work in our hearts....

Those who live in the same Spirit as the prophets and the apostles appreciate Scripture. George Fox explained his own experience: "I had no slight esteem of the Holy Scriptures, but they were very precious to me, for I was in that spirit by which they were given forth, and what the Lord opened in me I afterwards found was agreeable to them" (*Journal*, p. 34). Indeed, the Scriptures contain the words of God and therefore are very precious to us, but even more precious is the Word of God, Jesus Christ our Lord and Teacher, who opens the Bible to us.

DISCUSSION QUESTIONS:

1. Have you experienced the Scriptures as a check on revelations you've experienced that you realized were in error or misperceived? If so, share the story.
2. Are you troubled by some passages in the Scriptures and puzzled by others? Cite some examples. Friends believe that Christ Jesus can "open" the true meaning of Scripture to help people deal with troubling or puzzling passages, but that Christ may deem it neither necessary nor important that you understand something "right now." Is this a relief to you or do you chafe at not knowing what you would like to be able to understand or explain to others?
3. How does the original Quaker understanding of continuing revelation help us avoid undermining our entire faith and practice, and throwing us into confusion? How does a theory of continuing revelation in which "new truth" scotches or trumps "old truth," destroy any ground for clear faith and consistent witness?

Section 2.B
Are the Scriptures Essential to Salvation?

Readings: Terry H.S. Wallace, "Scripture and Salvation: To those who say that the Scriptures are inessential to our salvation"; Robert Barclay, *Apology for the True Christian Divinity*, Prop. 3, § V-VI (Freiday).

Salvation begins when we realize that we are poor, helpless people and seek God's help to obey Him, both in setting aside what we should not do and in doing what we should. George Fox's coming out of his spiritual wilderness and into God's kingdom meant giving himself up to the Lord in a whole series of acts—leaving evil company, taking leave of his relations, and setting aside outward supports to rely wholly on the Lord. Fox's moment of hope flashes forth when he faces his own helplessness: "When all my hopes ... in all men were gone, so that I had nothing outwardly to help me, nor could tell what to do, then, Oh then, I heard a voice which said, 'There is one, even Christ Jesus, that can speak to thy condition,' and when I heard it my heart did leap for joy" (*Journal*, p. 11). For Fox, Scripture could not do what our present Lord did, for living in the presence of, and at the direction of, our Lord is the work of salvation. Fox observes:

> Though I read the Scriptures that spoke of Christ and of God, yet I knew Him not but [except] by revelation, as he who hath the key did open[4], and as the Father of life drew me to his Son by his spirit. And then the Lord did gently lead me along, and did let me see his love, which was endless and eternal, and surpasseth the knowledge that men have in the natural [human] state, or can get by history or books;

---

[4] A Biblical allusion to Revelation 3:7.

and that love let me see myself as I was without him (*Journal*, p. 11-12).

In addition to testifying that an individual's personal salvation experience happens through Christ, early Friends understood that Christ enlightens all people, and thereby leads into salvation even people who do not have access to the Christian Scriptures. Of course, early Friends did have the Christian Scriptures, but although they used them extensively, early Friends did not claim the Scriptures to be "essential" to spiritual salvation. God's power and love are the essentials of salvation; where there is no Bible, God's power can still reach and save men and women. The Old and New Testaments are living witnesses to this fact: God's power was already working to direct men and women and to save them, before the Testaments existed. Today, too many people dismiss the Scriptures by drawing the unexamined conclusion that "inessential" means "useless," "of little value," and "can be readily skipped and ignored." They take what they think is the shortcut, which is actually the very long, circuitous, difficult, and dangerous route.

Terry Wallace explores several dangers of too casually asserting the "inessential" nature of the Scriptures for being saved from the World.

> First, we can too easily become centered on our individual experiences with Scripture and our own experiences of being drawn to Christ Jesus. While our witness to our own rescue from the World can be useful to a point, it can also lead us inadvertently to equate our experience as the common or even universal experience of men and women today. Yes, some do find that early on in their lives they are turned off by Scripture or have no significant acquaintance with it and yet Christ Jesus leads them along until they are finally open to Him, engaged with Him, and have passages of the Bible opened to them by His Spirit. Yet many others have grown

up with an appreciation and love of the Scriptures. The use of a word like "inessential" to describe the Scriptures will simply move to many of those people to reject what we have to say, because they are aware of how significant (this is not to say "sufficient") the Scriptures have been in their own salvation and sanctification.

Second, we must be sensitive to how others than ourselves may read and respond to the words we are using. We live in a time in which the World denigrates Scripture, ridicules it, and seeks to dismiss it. After all, its words from God stand too often as a judgment against the World's evil actions, destructive politics, lack of responsibility and self-control. If we say that the Scriptures are "inessential" to salvation, the ready response of fallen human nature is "Good! I don't have to deal with them...."

[Third, we] must be most careful in the words we use, because we should not imply that the gospels and the words of our Lord are "inessential"; that our Lord's life, crucifixion, sacrifice, and resurrection are "not required"; that, if such knowledge is "not required" and "insufficient" for our salvation, we may ignore them completely and consign them to the ash heap of history. Certainly, these are the easy spins the World can put on our words, spins that point out where our words might lead others.

Fourth,... [in] our haste to define what is essential to salvation, we risk inadvertently throwing into the negative much of what the Lord has given us to assist us in finding and walking on the straight and narrow Way....

Rather than an inessential impediment, the Scriptures are a God-given gift to help us seek and find Him, but they are not absolutely essential to salvation.

DISCUSSION QUESTIONS:

1. Generations of Quakers declared that the good news was God's power to save us. Why is God's power the essential point, rather than the Scriptures?
2. When does our salvation begin?
3. While the Scriptures may not be termed absolutely essential to salvation, why should they be declared as tremendously helpful, a roadmap help to avoid a host of problems and impediments to our spiritual lives, and a key encouragement and guide in our quest for salvation?
4. What particular impediments do you see to our spiritual search for salvation when we lack any knowledge of the Scriptures?

Section 2.C
Ways of Exploring the Bible

A person may become more acquainted with the Bible in many ways. Although some people simply start at the beginning of the Bible and read straight through, one has to be quite dedicated to complete that task. A modification of that method, which allows some choice of order, is to choose and read through one book of the Bible, followed by choosing and reading another. Alternatively, published guides that offer daily selections of related passages are available, allowing one to read the entire Bible in some number of years. Another method, which gives the Holy Spirit more immediate influence, is to open the book with little or no planning, perhaps aiming for some section such as the Psalms or the New Testament, and then read what one sees. Various Friends have borne testimony to the amazing efficacy of this last method, as they have found encouragement or answers to immediate problems embedded within the passage to which they opened.

Any of those methods for individual reading can also be profitably used by more than one adult at home, among two or three close friends, or with a few coworkers during a break at work. Establishing a regular daily time for Bible reading helps ward off competing demands for one's attention. Depending on the people involved and the time available, discussing what has been read may or may not be helpful.

Parents sometimes inquire how they can share the Bible with their children. The method chosen depends, of course, on the children's reading and comprehension abilities. Including a book of children's Bible stories among the other books read to young children makes a natural beginning. Some such children's Bible books are more consistent with Friends' beliefs than others. When children reach school age, the family can join together to read aloud from the Bible itself. Everyone can take a turn in choosing a selection or reading verses. Talking about the meaning of the story read and its application to present situations adds life to the process.

In addition to reading the Bible privately, within the family, and with a few other people, Friends often appreciate reading the Bible as a meeting function. Again, there are various methods. Some groups choose a published guide to Scripture study, which includes interpretive readings and questions for discussion. Other groups move more on their own, starting with one book of the Bible and taking turns reading aloud. Each reader stops after several verses, allowing opportunity for any Friends who feel so moved to tell what meaning those verses have for them. When discussion on one section seems finished, the next person reads another short section. A third method for group Bible reading involves no discussion at all, bypassing possibilities for contention and leaving the Holy Spirit to work within each person. In this way, Friends gather in silence, as in an unprogrammed meeting for worship. As individual Friends feel led, various ones read aloud a passage they have found. Ample time should be allowed between readers for everyone's silent consideration of what has been read and to allow the Holy Spirit to "open" what has been read.

Some of the ways of reading the Bible emphasize intellectual analysis, while others use a more spiritual approach. Although academic discipline is useful in examination of religious scriptures and of our relationship to them, an entirely intellectual perspective on Scripture blocks the spiritual dimension of the Bible. For those of us trained to rely on logical thinking, it is difficult to shift out of an intellectual frame of reference. Nevertheless, in order to make use of all that the Bible offers, we need to be led beyond rational analysis into feeling the Bible's spiritual direction. When the Bible is used without the Holy Spirit's immediate guidance, spiritual growth will be absent and harm may be done, either to the person involved or to someone else. Any such hurt inflicted can be resolved not through rejection of either the harmful person or the Bible, but through returning to the renewing power of God.

DISCUSSION QUESTIONS:

1. What has been your personal experience of the Scriptures?
2. How do the Scriptures facilitate transcending our individual experiences and intellect?
3. How do the Scriptures help us communicate with one another?
4. How do the Scriptures help Christ communicate with us?
5. How might we misuse the Scriptures?
6. How do we know right from wrong use of the Scriptures?
7. What is resonating most deeply within you?

Section 2.D
The Psalms and Other Scripture Passages

One part of the Bible through which people often find a personal connection with God is the book of Psalms. Reading a favorite psalm, or opening somewhere in that book and reading whatever appears, can be a very effective beginning for a time of private devotion. Psalm 121, for example, establishes the importance of looking to God: "I will lift up my eyes to the hills. From where does my help come? My help comes from God, who made heaven and earth...." Psalm 100 reminds us of God's goodness: "For the Lord is good; his mercy is everlasting; and his truth continues to all generations." Woven throughout much of the Psalms is an insistence that God alone be worshipped, and that trusting in other gods leads away from peace and into confusion (e.g. Psalm 97:7). Depression and despair also find ample expression in the Psalms: "My heart is smitten and withered like grass, so that I forget to eat.... I have mingled my drink with weeping." (Psalm 102: 4, 9) However, the psalms continually affirm that God acts with mercy and love: "Praise the Lord, oh my soul, and forget not all God's benefits ... who redeems your life from destruction, who crowns you with love and tender compassion.... The Lord is compassionate and gracious, slow to anger and abounding in love." (Psalm 103: 2, 4, 8)

Not only in Psalms but also throughout the rest of the Bible, passages reach beyond historical or doctrinal statements to give voice to the spiritual conditions and longings of each of us. Whether a particular passage has spiritual significance at a given time depends on the immediate state of the reader or hearer. A section that is meaningless one day may be deeply significant a few days later under different spiritual circumstances, or it may take years before the reader gains insight into the passage's spiritual significance. Similarly, a section that means a lot at one reading can open into additional, even entirely new dimensions later on.

Some passages that Friends have often found speaking to their particular condition include:

> O sing unto the Lord a new song; sing unto the Lord, all the earth ... for the Lord is great and greatly to be praised.... Let the heavens rejoice, and let the earth be glad. (Psalm 96: 1, 4, 11)

> Come, all you who are thirsty, come to the waters, and you who have no money, come, buy and eat! Come, buy wine and milk without money and without cost. Why spend money on what is not bread, and your labor on what does not satisfy? Listen, listen to me, and eat what is good, and your soul will delight in the richest of fare. (Isaiah 55:1-2)

> Blessed are those who mourn, for they will be comforted. Blessed are the meek, for they will inherit the earth. Blessed are the merciful, for they will be shown mercy. (Matthew 5: 4, 5, 7; also the other Beatitudes)

> The wolf will live with the lamb, the leopard will lie down with the goat, the calf and the lion and the yearling together, and a little child will lead them.... They will neither harm nor destroy on all my holy mountain. (Isaiah 11:6, 9)

> I will praise you, O Lord. Although you were angry with me, your anger has turned away and you have comforted me. Surely God is my salvation; I will trust and not be afraid. (Isaiah 12:1-2)

> Trust in the Lord with all your heart, and lean not on your own understanding. In all your ways acknowledge him, and he will direct your path. (Proverbs 3:5-6)

For unto us a child is born, unto us a son is given, and the government shall be upon his shoulder. And his name shall be called Wonderful, Counselor, the mighty God, the everlasting Father, the Prince of Peace. (Isaiah 9:6)

This is the covenant I will make with the house of Israel after that time, declares the Lord. I will put my laws in their minds and write them on their hearts. I will be their God, and they will be my people. No longer will a man teach his neighbor, or a man his brother, saying, 'Know the Lord,' because they will all know me, from the least of them to the greatest. For I will forgive their wickedness and will remember their sins no more. (Jeremiah 31:33-34; Hebrews 8:10-12)

And this is God's command: to believe in the name of his Son Jesus Christ, and to love one another. Those who obey God's commands live in God, and God lives in them. This is how we know: we know by the Spirit God gave us. (1 John 3:23-24)

I [John] baptize you with water for repentance. But after me will come one who is more powerful than I, whose sandals I am not fit to carry. He will baptize you with the Holy Spirit and fire. (Matthew 3:11)

All things have been committed to me by my Father. No one knows the Son except the Father, and no one knows the Father except the Son and those to whom the Son chooses to reveal him. (Matthew 11:27)

For where two or three are gathered together in my name, there am I in the midst of them. (Matthew 18:20)

In the beginning was the Word, and the Word was with God, and the Word was God. He was with God in the beginning. Through him all things were made; without him nothing was made that has been made. In him was life, and that life was the light of men. The light shines in the darkness, but the darkness has not understood.... This was the true light that gives light to every man who comes into the world. (John 1:1-5, 9)

Jesus said to them, "I tell you the truth, it is not Moses who has given you the bread from heaven, but it is my Father who gives you the true bread from heaven. For the bread of God is he who comes down from heaven and gives life to the world." "Sir," they said, "from now on give us this bread." Then Jesus declared, "I am the bread of life. He who comes to me will never go hungry, and he who believes in me will never be thirsty. (John 6:32-35)

But the Counselor, the Holy Spirit, whom the Father will send in my name, will teach you all things and will remind you of everything I have said to you. (John 14:26)

Remain in me, and I will remain in you. No branch can bear fruit by itself; it must remain in the vine. Neither can you bear fruit unless you remain in me. (John 15:4)

You are my friends if you do what I command. I no longer call you servants, because a servant does not know his master's business. Instead, I have called you friends, for everything that I learned from my Father I have made known to you. You did not choose me, but I chose you and appointed you to go and bear fruit—fruit that will last. (John 15:14-16)

[And Jesus said, to them] wait for the gift my Father promised, which you have heard me speak about. For John baptized with water, but in a few days you will be baptized with the Holy Spirit. (Acts 1:4-5)

[T]his is what was spoken by the prophet Joel: "In the last days, God says, I will pour out my Spirit on all people. Your sons and daughters will prophesy, your young men will see visions, your old men will dream dreams." (Acts 2:16-17)

The Spirit himself testifies with our spirit that we are God's children. (Romans 8:16)

But what does it say? "The Word is near you; it is in your mouth and in your heart," that is, the Word of faith we are proclaiming. (Romans 10:8)

Christ did not send me to baptize, but to preach the gospel—not with words of human wisdom, lest the cross of Christ be emptied of its power. (1 Corinthians 1:17)

But he who unites himself with the Lord is one with him in spirit. (1 Corinthians 6:17)

Now to each one the manifestation of the Spirit is given for the common good. (1 Corinthians 12:7 [NIV])

For we were all baptized by one Spirit into one body—whether Jews or Greeks, slave or free—and we were all given the one Spirit to drink. (1 Corinthians 12:13)

Examine yourselves to see whether you are in the faith; test yourselves. Do you not realize that Christ Jesus is in you—unless, of course, you fail your test? (2 Corinthians 13:5)

There is one body and one Spirit—just as you were called to one hope when you were called—one Lord, one faith, one baptism; one God and Father of all, who is over all and through all and in all. (Ephesians 4:4-6)

But everything exposed by the light becomes visible, for it is light that makes everything visible. (Ephesians 5:13-14)

To them God has chosen to make known among the Gentiles the glorious riches of this mystery, which is Christ in you, the hope of glory. (Colossians 1:27)

For the grace of God that brings salvation has appeared to all men. (Titus 2:11)

Make every effort to live in peace with all men and to be holy; without holiness no one will see the Lord. (Hebrews 12:14)

This is the message we have heard from him and declare to you: God is light; in him there is no darkness at all. If we claim to have fellowship with him yet walk in the darkness, we lie and do not live by the truth. But if we walk in the light, as he is in the light, we have fellowship with one another, and the blood of Jesus, his Son, purifies us from all sin. (1 John 1:5-7)

Do not love the world or anything in the world. If anyone loves the world, the love of the Father is not in him. For everything in the world—the cravings of sinful man, the lust of his eyes and the boasting of what he has and does—comes not from the Father but from the world. The world and its desires pass away, but the man who does the will of God lives forever. (1 John 2:15-17)

Familiarity with the Scriptures does not happen all at once, but even a small beginning can have positive spiritual as well as cognitive effects. Internalizing those few verses listed above from the 96th Psalm, for example, provides a person with ready words of rejoicing and praise when even small blessings are encountered. Recalling a few phrases from the 23rd Psalm ("The Lord is my shepherd; I shall not want....") offers encouragement to trust God under stress. Living in and nurturing our own spiritual responsiveness in daily situations opens the door to God's work in our lives. In turn, as we allow God to work within us, we become more able to tap into the resources for growth in both knowledge and faith, which God has provided within the Bible. And, as we become more in tune with God's purposes, we are further enabled to reach out to others in ways pleasing to God.

The Bible, taken in its entirety, presents a description of God's call to humanity to listen to God and to respond with faith, to confess our human inabilities and to surrender to God's love, to recognize that God's love is made known to us through God's Son Jesus Christ, and then to share that love with our neighbors, wherever we find them. Although the essence of this message is simple, fully comprehending its complexities is beyond the ability of any individual person. Nevertheless, we are drawn by the power of God into faithfulness to God and thence into unity with each other. The Bible is a useful tool for directing our thoughts into a clearer understanding of God's purposes, for finding words to express our inherent spiritual desires, and for shaping our responses to God's work within us.

DISCUSSION QUESTIONS:

1. Which other Bible passages have you found helpful and inspiring? How so?
2. How and how often do you use the Bible?
3. If you do not use it much, what prevents you from using it more?
4. What is resonating most with you?

Chapter 3
THE INWARD LIFE

Section 3.A
The Spiritual Search

Readings: Matthew 11:27; John 10:1-5; 17:3; Robert Barclay, APOLOGY FOR THE TRUE CHRISTIAN DIVINITY Prop. 1 (Freiday)

Unworthiness, Weariness, and Doubt. Robert Barclay begins the *Apology* with John 17:3: "Now this is eternal life: that they may know you, the only true God, and Jesus Christ, whom you have sent" (NIV). Barclay then describes the search for knowing God.

> A man first proposes to know God when his conscience brings about a sense of his own unworthiness, and a great weariness of mind is unwittingly affected by the gentle yet real glances of God's light upon him. The earnest desires he has to be redeemed from his present troubles make him tender in heart and ready to receive impression. He desires to be freed from his disordered passions and lusts and to find quietness and peace in the certain knowledge of God, and in the assurance of God's love and goodwill toward him. Since he has not yet achieved clear discernment, he is eager to embrace anything that will alleviate his present condition.
>
> If he centers himself on certain principles at that stage, it will be very difficult to alter these opinions no matter how wrong they may be. These first opinions are often arrived at through respect for certain persons, or unconscious compliance with his own natural disposition. Once the first anguish is over, he becomes more hardy, and a false peace and certain confidence is created. The enemy is near and is strengthened by the unwillingness of the mind to resume its doubts or the anxiety of searching. How much more difficult

to bring him then to enter the right way, if he has missed his road at the beginning of the journey and was mistaken in his first guideposts.

Barclay concludes that "No one knows the Father except the Son and those to whom the Son chooses to reveal him" (Matthew 11:27). Christ Jesus seeks to save all people, but it is each person's decision to embrace or reject His revelation of Himself.

DISCUSSION QUESTIONS:

1. Barclay says that a sense of unworthiness is the consequence of the glances of God's Light. In your experience, how else may a search for God begin? Does it matter how the search begins?
2. Barclay describes the peace of knowing God as being freed from disordered passions and lusts. What evidence can we point to that our passions are disordered? What does it mean to have a rightly ordered life?
3. Barclay warns of accepting spiritual principles that comply with our personal dispositions. How do we know when we are accepting principles because they are consistent with our preexisting personality and when we are accepting principles because they are consistent with Christ's personality?
4. Barclay warns against a false hardiness, peace, and confidence. Can you give examples of such false hardiness, peace, and confidence that you've experienced or seen?
5. Barclay warns that the enemy can be strengthened by our unwillingness to resume our doubts. Are all doubts inspired by the Holy Spirit? Who is the enemy?
6. What is resonating most deeply within you?

*All Friends wait in the measure of the Spirit of God
to guide you up to God.*
~ George Fox

Section 3.B
Inward States, Dryness, and the Daily Cross

Readings: *The Journal of George Fox* (John L. Nickalls, ed.), Chs. 1-2, 4

They, they, they, I, I, I. George Fox explained how we fail to see the evil within us, locating it instead outside of us:

> And I saw the state of those, both priests and people, who, in reading the Scriptures, cry out much against Cain, Esau, and Judas and other wicked men of former times mentioned in the Holy Scriptures, but do not see the nature of Cain, of Esau, and of Judas, and those others, in themselves. And these said it was they, they, they, who were the bad people, putting it off from themselves: but when some of these came with the light and spirit of Truth to see themselves, then they came to say, "I, I, I, it is I myself that has been the Ishmael, and the Esau," etc. For then they came to see the nature of wild Ishmael in themselves, the nature of Cain, of Esau, of Korah, of Balaam, and of the son of perdition in themselves, sitting above all that is called God in them [p. 30].

Friends understand that in addition to their historical significance, the persons and situations in the Scriptures reveal spiritual states and struggles. Thus, there is a spiritual state of Judas in which we may find ourselves, over and above the historical Judas who betrayed Jesus of Nazareth. Indeed, the biblical story from Genesis through Revelation can be read as a road map to the spiritual life of Christians—that the spiritual development of a Christian follows much of the story line of the Bible.

Dryness. Fox explains why a previously powerful meeting had come to dryness:

> And the next day I passed to Cleveland amongst those people that had tasted the power of God, but were all shattered to pieces and the heads of them [some of their leaders] had turned Ranters.[5] Now they had had great meetings, so I told them after that they had had such meetings they did not wait upon God to feel his power to gather their minds together to feel his presence and power and therein to sit to wait upon him, for they had spoken themselves dry and had spent their portions and not lived in that which they spake, and now they were dry [p. 79].

Daily Cross. Fox explained the power of God:

> Therefore keep in the daily cross, the power of God, by which ye may witness all that to be crucified which is contrary to the will of God, and which shall not come into his kingdom [p. 18].

DISCUSSION QUESTIONS:

1. So long as the "priests and people" continued to see evil in others, they were lost. It was only by the "light and spirit of Truth" that some came to be able to see the evil nature within themselves. Why does it require the intervention of the Light of Christ for us to see our own darkness?

---

[5] Ranters were a vague seventeenth century group. They claimed the indwelling Spirit, rejected outward religious forms, believed in each individual's understanding of the Spirit, and accepted immoral activity, if it were done "in the Spirit." Ranters lacked Friends' emphasis on Christian self-denial, holiness, and the conviction of being a gathered people—governed by the Holy Spirit with a shared sense of right gospel order.

2. Do you find the idea that the spiritual development of a Christian follows much of the story line of the Bible helpful? Give examples of how it is helpful to you.
3. The daily cross is defined as the power of God. How does God's power crucify that which is contrary to His will? Can you give examples from your own experience of the daily cross crucifying ungodly passions and desires within you?
4. What do you think Fox means when he says "come into his kingdom"?
5. What do the Scriptures say about those who have tasted the power of God but turned away? Hebrews 6:4-8; 2 Peter 2:15-22. Why does anyone turn away?
6. How does not living in God's will bring us to spiritual dryness? Can you cite examples from your life or the lives of others?
7. What is resonating most deeply within you?

Section 3.C
The Unchangeable Teacher, Prophet, Shepherd

Readings: *The Journal of George Fox* (John L. Nickalls, ed.), Chs. 1, 6.

Brittle and changeable. George Fox describes the consequences of seeking after changeable things and uncertain teachers:

> But while people's minds do run in the earthly, after the creatures and changeable things, and changeable ways, and religions, and changeable, uncertain teachers, their minds are in bondage. And they are brittle and changeable, and tossed up and down with windy doctrines and thoughts, and notions and things, their minds being [away] from the unchangeable truth in the inward parts, the light of Jesus Christ, which would keep their minds to the unchangeable, who is the way to the Father, who in all my troubles did preserve me by his spirit and power (*Journal*, p.13).

Roles of Christ. George Fox explains different roles of Christ in the Christian life:

> And I brought them all to the spirit of God in themselves, by which they might know God and Christ and the Scriptures and to have heavenly fellowship in the spirit; and showed them how every one that comes into the world was enlightened by Christ the life, with which light they might see their sins and Christ their savior, who has come to save them from their sin; with which light they might see their priest that died for them, their shepherd to feed them, and their great prophet to open to them. So with the light of Christ they might see Christ always present with them, who was the author of their faith and the finisher thereof.... [I

showed them how] Christ was come to teach his people himself and how they might find their teacher within, when they were in their labors and in their beds (*Journal*, p.155).

DISCUSSION QUESTIONS:

1. Have you experienced being in "bondage" to "changeable" ways and teachers? How did it make you "brittle?" What is it to be "tossed up and down with windy doctrines"?
2. What is your experience of being preserved in "his spirit and power" in spite of troubles?
3. What is your experience of the unchangeable?
4. Friends believe that everyone who comes into the world is enlightened by Christ (John 1:9). However, not everyone is committed to following this Light. Why? What are the consequences?
5. Friends emphasize that Christ has other roles (or "offices") in addition to being "savior," which is the role most professing Christians emphasize. What does it mean for Christ to be our "shepherd," "teacher" and "prophet?" What does it mean for Christ to be the "author" and "finisher" of faith?
6. Fox repeatedly says that Christ has come to teach "his people" himself. The reference to "people" is obviously a reference to people as a group. Have you experienced Christ Jesus teaching an entire group of His people? Please describe the experience.
7. What is resonating most deeply within you?

*But the Counselor, the Holy Spirit,
whom the Father will send in my name,
will teach you all things and will remind you of everything
I have said to you.
~ John 14:26*

*This is the covenant I will make
with the house of Israel after that time, declares the Lord.
I will put my laws in their minds and write them on their hearts.
I will be their God, and they will be my people.
No longer will a man teach his neighbor,
or a man his brother, saying, 'Know the Lord,'
because they will all know me, from the least of them to the greatest.
~ Hebrews 8:10-11; Jeremiah 31:33-34*

*As for you, the anointing you received from him remains in you,
and you do not need anyone to teach you.
But as his anointing teaches you about all things and as that anointing is real,
not counterfeit -- just as it has taught you, remain in him
~ 1 John 2:27*

Section 3.D
"I Heard A Voice...."

Readings: *The Journal of George Fox* (John L. Nickalls, ed.), Ch. 1.

Experiencing God's Voice. In the opening pages of George Fox's *Journal*, he describes his frustration and desperation as he searched from one religious group to the next, one religious leader to the next looking for the truth. He writes:

> And when all my hopes in them and in all men were gone, so that I had nothing outwardly to help me, nor could tell what to do, then, oh then, I heard a voice which said, "There is one, even Christ Jesus, that can speak to thy condition," and when I heard it my heart did leap for joy. Then the Lord did let me see why there was none upon the earth that could speak to my condition, namely that I might give him all the glory.... And this I knew experimentally [*Journal of George Fox* (Nickalls edition), p. 11].

This experience was the turning point in Fox's personal life. He understood his life work to be helping to bring others to the experience of Christ speaking to them—and then leaving them there. This short passage contains at least three important ideas. 1) The first is the intense nature of true spiritual seeking. Fox had been exhausted by his spiritual seeking. He had given up hope. He was not in a state of self-satisfaction, comfort, or confidence. Early Friends' journals often record struggles, pain, and darkness. Their spiritual search was a matter of urgency and desperation. It was very serious. It was life and death. 2) The second is that Christ Jesus speaks directly to our own personal condition. 3) The third is that either we have personally experienced Christ's Voice—or we have not. Second-hand knowledge will not do, nor will speculation. It is not a matter of theology. It is a matter of experience.

DISCUSSION QUESTIONS:

1. Friends' journals often record spiritual struggles of an intensity rarely heard today. Why might that be?
2. Some experience a dramatic awakening or conversion, while others have a gentler experience. Why? What has been your experience?
3. Have you experienced Christ Jesus speaking to your condition? Please give an example. How was your experience different from merely being pricked by a pang of conscience or experiencing an "imagination"?
4. What is resonating most deeply within you?

Have but few books, but let them be well chosen and well read, whether of religious or civil subjects. Shun fantastic opinions; measure both religion and learning by practice; reduce all to that, for that brings a real benefit to you; the rest is a thief and a snare. And indeed, reading many books is but a taking off the mind too much from meditation. Reading yourselves and nature, in the dealings and conduct of men, is the truest human wisdom. The spirit of a man knows the things of man, and more true knowledge comes by meditation and just reflection than by reading; for much reading is an oppression of the mind, and extinguishes the natural candle, which is the reason of so many senseless scholars in the world.
~ William Penn

Section 3.E
Spiritual Baptism

Readings: Matthew 3:11, 10:38-39; Mark 1:8, 16:16; Luke 3:16; John 4:2; Acts 1:5, 11:16; Romans 6:3-14; 1 Corinthians 1:14-17, 10:2; Galatians 3:27; Ephesians 4:5; 1 Peter 3:21; Robert Barclay, *Apology for the True Christian Divinity*, Prop. 12

What is baptism? Baptism means "immersion." The word "baptism" is used in several senses in the Scriptures. In fact, water baptism is an old Jewish ceremony used in the induction of new members. This ancient rite was the origin of the baptism practiced by John the Baptist, as John notes when he emphasizes that "After me comes the one more powerful than I, the straps of whose sandals I am not worthy to stoop down and untie. I baptize you with water, but he will baptize you with the Holy Spirit" (Mark 1:7-8). The latter baptism is Christ's baptism, the baptism of the New Covenant spoken of in Ephesians 4:5: "There is one body and one Spirit—just as you were called to one hope when you were called—one Lord, one faith, one baptism; one God and Father of all, who is over all and through all and in all." Each of us is visited by our Lord. He calls upon us to repent of our disobedience to Him and turn to Him. God says, "Here I am! I stand at the door and knock. If anyone hears my voice and opens the door, I will go in and eat with him, and he with me" (Rev.3:20). This repentance and opening to God is the beginning of our immersion in the life of the Spirit.

The result of our responding to God leads to a spiritual birth into holiness and a new life. As Peter instructs in 1 Peter 1:13+: "Prepare your minds for action; be self-controlled; set your hope fully on the grace to be given you when Jesus Christ is revealed." We are to live our lives as strangers to the world, in reverent fear and having "purified" ourselves "by obeying the truth so that you have sincere love for your brothers, love one another deeply, with all your hearts." "We have been born again, not of perishable seed, but of imperishable, through the living and enduring word of God" (1 Peter 1:22-23).

This turning of ourselves to God is the work of the Holy Spirit. It is *not* mere intellectual agreement with certain doctrines, but a spiritual transformation of our whole self, so that we become wholly oriented towards the Holy Spirit to teach us (John 14:26), speak through us (Acts 2:4), and guide us (Romans 8:9). We may have been taught and accepted various true and helpful doctrines, but doing so is not sufficient to make us Christian. Rather, we can only answer to the Spirit of God in clarity and peace after we have experienced this baptism, this immersion in the Spirit, this inward washing with fire, this melting of our inward self that leaves us open to do the Spirit's will.

Such an inward baptism takes many forms. Robert Barclay described his baptismal transformation as an inward warming of the heart. For George Fox, it was hearing a voice that said: "There is one, even Christ Jesus, who can speak to thy condition." He began listening and his entire life was altered. However, depending on how recalcitrant, wrong, or wicked one's former life was, the visitation of the Spirit may be at first more devastating, as it was for Saul on the road to Damascus, struck down and blinded for a time by his meeting with his Lord.

Baptism and the Cross. Quakers understand that we are baptized by, and thus led by, the Holy Spirit to take up our cross so that we can fully die to self—and thereby live in Christ. This description of baptism's relation to the cross is found in the Scriptures, too (1 Corinthians 1:17).

Baptism and true conversion. What is the true outward sign of an inward grace? Water baptism cannot be the outward sign of a Christian, because it does not convey the Spirit. The sign of a true

Christian conversion is a life that bears spiritual fruit (Matthew 7:16-20; John 15; Galatians 5:22-24). The requirement of a Christian life is to take up the cross of Christ and bear the fruits of His Spirit. Unlike the passing and inconsistent references to water baptism in the Scriptures, this requirement is wholly clear in them. After all, millions have received a so-called water baptism, but far fewer have shown forth the fruits of the Spirit's baptism.

DISCUSSION QUESTIONS:

1. What are your experiences of spiritual baptism? How are they similar or different to the experiences described in the Scriptures or by others (such as early Friends)?
2. What signs might we see in a person undergoing God's baptism?
3. What signs might we see in a person baptized by the Holy Spirit?
4. How often does a person need to be spiritually baptized? Why?
5. How can we best communicate why we reject water baptism?
6. What is resonating most deeply within you?

Section 3.F
Spiritual Communion

Readings: Matthew 26:26-29; Mark 14:22-25; Luke 22:17-20; John 6:35-48; 1 Corinthians 11:17-34; Romans 14; Robert Barclay, *Apology for the True Christian Divinity*, Prop. 13.

The experience of Christ Jesus, for Quakers, is direct, immediate, and intimate. Such an experience can happen among worshippers assembled together for worship and through the individual experience of Christ's presence in daily life. While Roman Catholics refer to the Real Presence of Jesus Christ in the bread and wine of the Eucharist, Quakers recognize and experience His Real Presence both in meetings for worship and in their daily walk communing with Him. The first generation Quaker apostle, Edward Burrough (1634-1662), testified thus as to the worship of God: "The worship of God in itself is this: It is a walking with God, and a living with Him in converse and fellowship, in spirit and truth, for He is only worshipped therein—and to do the truth and speak the truth. This is the true worship of God, where the mind is guided with the Spirit of Truth, and the presence of the Lord felt at all times, and His fear in the hearts of people, and His counsel stood in, and His covenant felt, which united to the Lord in Spirit. This is the true worship of God—and it is without respect to times or things" (*The Memorable Works of a Son of Thunder and Consolation...*, London: 1672, 474).

The last supper Jesus shared with His disciples was certainly not the first, or only, time He shared this understanding with His disciples. It was but one of the ways He emphasized His command that we allow Him to abide in us and that we abide in Him (John 15:5). The understanding of Christ Jesus as our spiritual food is emphasized repeatedly beyond the confines of the last supper and is a description of our relationship to Christ in biological images, like

John 15's branch-to-vine description or Paul's descriptions of the body of Christ (Romans, 12: 3-8; 1 Corinthians 12; Colossians 1:18).

Communion in meeting for worship. When we live in spiritual communion with Jesus Christ, we often experience that communion most clearly during meetings for worship. Indeed, we may understand our meetings for worship as meetings for communion. Friends may use terms like *covered meeting* or *gathered meeting* to describe a meeting for worship in which the experience of spiritual communion with Christ is exceptionally deep. Friends also use the term *centered* to describe the exceptional experience of being focused intensely on the Presence of Christ and our relationship with Him. While these terms are most commonly used to describe experiences of meetings for worship, neither spiritual communion nor these experiences are limited to such meetings, just as worship itself is not.

Ceremonial communion. Friends do not condemn those who "from a true tenderness of spirit and with real conscience towards God," imitate the Last Supper (Barclay Proposition 13, Section XI). However, Friends see living in spiritual communion with Jesus as the essence of communion, making ceremonial communion unnecessary.

Love feasts. Scriptural references in the New Testament to Christians "breaking bread" together are not descriptions of ceremonial communion, but rather references to fellowship meals or love feasts. No ceremonial or ritualistic details are ever described (see Acts 2:42, 2:46, 20:7, 20:11, 27:35). As Robert Barclay explained, these early Christians were eating together in true Christian fellowship, "being together not merely to feed their bellies," but "to eat and drink together in the dread and presence of the Lord, as His people" (Barclay, Proposition 13, Section VIII, 353). Such love feasts, when misunderstood, could devolve into degraded gatherings quite the opposite of fellowship meals, gatherings characterized by selfishness, gluttony, drunkenness and cliquishness. Paul, in 1 Corinthians 11:17-34, describes such an instance in which the Corinthian church was gathering merely to fill their stomachs, rather than gathering as the Lord's people in awareness of His Presence and in love for one another.

DISCUSSION QUESTIONS:

1. What are the underlying differences between a religious approach that considers issues by what individuals find meaningful and one that seeks to determine what God desires?
2. How might we expect people to act as they emerge from a gathered meeting for worship, where communion with God has been rich and deep?
3. Can individual Friends be in that kind of communion with God outside meeting for worship? If so, where? When? And how?
4. What is your experience of spiritual communion?
5. What is resonating most deeply within you?

Section 3.G
Discerning Leadings

Readings: Hugh Barbour, *Five Tests for Discerning a True Leading.*

Early Friends faced the daily job of recognizing the true from the subjective when they felt led to speech and action. From Jeremiah's time to the present, men have known no absolute or easy way to tell a genuinely divine message from wishful impulses and false prophecy.

The problem was made urgent for the Quakers because they were regularly labeled by people of their time as "Ranters." The actual Ranters were a religious movement of the seventeenth century that superficially resembled the Friends and used much the same religious language. Ranters claimed that since they were redeemed and led by the Spirit, they could do no wrong, and so followed impulses into all kinds of immorality and anarchy. Some went further, saying that no man could be freed from a sin until he had committed that sin as if it were not a sin. Most of them felt they had found true faith or had been given a special prophetic call by God after a period of frustration in orthodox churches. Some were clearly psychotic. It was therefore important for Quakers to know themselves, to find a basis for guiding and disciplining one another when necessary, and to explain to others how they differed from Ranters.

While Friends emphasize being led by the Holy Spirit, they recognize that we are susceptible to the prince of lies, the spirit of deceit. Thus, the ability to discern a true leading from a false one is of great importance. Hugh Barbour described several tests Friends have used over the years for discerning whether a leading is truly of Christ Jesus.

1. MORAL PURITY. The first test for the genuineness of a leading was moral purity. Friends said that the Ranters "fled the cross," and that the true Spirit was always contrary to self-will and led to righteousness. They applied this test within their own groups, and their austerity was certainly in contrast to the libertine habits of the Ranters. Even condemnation of the impure was part of this test, "for the word of the Lord is pure," wrote George Fox in a reference to Jeremiah 23:28, "and answers the pure in everyone.... It is as a hammer to beat down the transgressor."

2. PATIENCE. As a second test, elders warned Friends to sit with their leadings for a while in patience. Self-will is impatient of tests. Fox wrote, "Be patient and still in the power and still in the light that doth convince you, keep your minds unto God.... If you sit still in the patience which overcomes in the power of God, there will be no flying."

3. CONSISTENCY WITH OTHERS. A third and most important test was likely to be the self-consistency of the Spirit. The Light should not contradict itself, either in history or among the members of the Spirit-led group. Even the senior preachers submitted their directives to each others' testing. In 1659, Thomas Aldam and William Dewsbury wrote to George Fox and Edward Burrough: "Take into your consideration the things written down in that power which came to me and W. Dew. at York and let me have an answer, how the large wisdom of God in you doth approve of the particular things to be done, and what it disapproves of, that in one mind we may meet." From these informal ways of verifying each others' leadings, there grew up in turn the practical processes of Quaker meetings for business. Sharing the Spirit of God within them underlay the deepest of all Quaker experiences, the unspoken awareness of the unification of the group by the Spirit in the silent meeting, where the whole body, and not primarily its individuals, received power, wisdom, and joy.

4. CONSISTENCY WITH THE BIBLE. One strong means for using the consistency of the Spirit as a test for the validity of leadings was to compare them with biblical statements. Friends were never willing to use the Bible directly as a guidebook or rule book lest it substitute for each person's own direct experience of the Light of Christ. In every area of life, the Spirit must be absolute. But the Quakers, of course, believed that the biblical writers were also divinely inspired and that biblical teachings and prophecies were therefore proper to use for comparison. They were also willing for their opponents to test them by the Bible. This agreement of the Spirit with the Bible was *recognized* more easily than it would be now, since early Friends were steeped in the Bible and its vocabulary.

DISCUSSION QUESTIONS:

1. How do we determine what is morally pure?
2. What is patience in the context of the sense of an immediate leading—for example, the sense to go visit someone right away?
3. In terms of consistency with others or the Bible, how do we address the risk that the "others" in our life are just as likely to be wrong as we are, or that our understanding of the Scriptures likely reflects our predispositions?
4. How do we distinguish compulsiveness, impulsiveness, obsessions, and our "normal interests" from leadings of the Holy Spirit?
5. How does each of the tests apply (or not apply) to speaking a message during meeting for worship?
6. What is resonating most deeply within you?

Section 3.H
"What Canst Thou Say?"

Readings: Margaret Fell, *A Sincere and Constant Love: An Introduction to the Work of Margaret Fell*, p. 174-186.

Margaret Fell's conviction. Margaret Fell was one of the key Quaker ministers and leaders. She recorded her experience of the first time she heard Fox preach, an event that led to her conversion and convincement of the Truth of his message:

> [Fox] went on, and said how Christ was the light of the world, and lights every man that comes into the world, and that by this light they might be gathered to God, etc. I stood up in my pew. I wondered at his doctrine, for I had never heard such before. Then he went on, and opened the Scriptures, and said: The Scriptures were the prophets' words, and Christ's and the apostles' words, and what, as they spoke, they enjoyed and possessed and had it from the Lord. [He] said, then what had any to do with the Scriptures, but as they came to the Spirit that gave them forth. "You will say, Christ says this, and the apostles say this, but what can you say? Are you a child of light, and have walked in the light? What you speak, is it inwardly from God?"
>
> This opened me so, that it cut me to the heart, and then I saw clearly we were all wrong. So I sat me down in my pew again, and cried bitterly. I cried in my spirit to the Lord, "We are all thieves, we are all thieves, we have taken the Scriptures in words, and know nothing of them in ourselves" (p. 176).

Fox's central challenge to Margaret Fell and the rest of the congregation at Ulverston was: "Do you actually possess the Life and

Spirit of Christ Jesus? Have you experienced His presence and responded to His inward leading? When you speak, are you bringing a message from our Lord, or simply mouthing words of your own or that you've picked up from others or from books or from the Scriptures? Do you actually possess the Spirit, or are you simply professing to be a Christian without having met and received Jesus Christ, the present and living Lord?" Margaret Fell was both stunned and shattered by Fox's challenge, because she realized that all her religious searching and striving for thirty-eight years had come to nothing. She had done what the church had told her to do, read the Scriptures, tried to keep the commandments, attended church, but had gained neither a sense of salvation nor the inner knowledge of Christ's presence. When Fox asked, *What canst thou say?*—he was not asking "What are your own creative thoughts and unusual experiences," but "Have you experienced what Christ, His apostles, and the prophets experienced and knew?" Margaret confessed she had the words, but not the spiritual reality and life of which they spoke. The good news that developed from this bitter realization is that she soon was open to the visitation and leading of the Spirit and could declare, "Yes! What I speak is inwardly from God! I am no longer a spiritual thief claiming the Life I do not have."

DISCUSSION QUESTIONS:

1. Have you had an experience similar to Margaret Fell's in which you realized that what you professed to be your faith was not inwardly from God? What followed that realization? Did it ultimately bring you closer to a sense of the presence of the living Christ?
2. Can you now declare, "What I speak is inwardly from God?" Why?

I will begin here also with the beginning of time in the morning. So soon as you wake, retire your mind into a pure silence from all thoughts and ideas of worldly things, and in that frame wait upon GOD, to feel His good presence, to lift up your hearts to Him, and commit your whole self into his blessed care and protection. Then rise, if well, immediately; being dressed, read a chapter or more in the Scriptures, and afterwards dispose yourselves for the business of the day, ever remembering that God is present, the overseer of all your thoughts, words, and actions, and demean [humble] yourselves, my dear children, accordingly, and do not you dare to do that in his holy, all-seeing presence, which you would be ashamed a man, yea, a child, should see you do. And as you have intervals from your lawful occasions, delight to step home (within yourselves, I mean), commune with your own hearts and be still. . .
~ *William Penn,* Advice to His Children, p.15

Section 3.I
"Be Still and Cool...."

Reading: *The Journal of George Fox* (John L. Nickalls, ed.), Ch. 15.

The letter to Lady Claypole. Oliver Cromwell was the "Protector" of the Puritan Revolution after King Charles I was beheaded. Cromwell, in reality, was thereafter the military dictator of England until his death in 1658. George Fox wrote the following to Lady Claypole (Oliver Cromwell's daughter) when she was "very sick and troubled in mind."

> Be still and cool in thy own mind and spirit from thy own thoughts, and then thou wilt feel the principle of God to turn thy mind to the Lord God, whereby thou wilt receive his strength and power from whence life comes, to allay all tempests, against blusterings and storms. That is it which moulds up into patience, into innocency, into soberness, into stillness, into stayedness, into quietness, up to God, with his power....

> Therefore be still a while from thy own thoughts, searching, seeking, desires and imaginations, and be stayed in the principle of God in thee, to stay thy mind upon God, up to God; and thou wilt find strength from him and find him to be a present help in time of trouble, in need, and to be a God at hand. And it will keep thee humble being come to the principle of God, which hath been transgressed.... There thou wilt come to receive and feel the physician of value, which clothes people in their right mind, whereby they may serve God and do his will.

For all distractions, distempers, unruliness, confusion are in the transgression; which transgression must be brought down, before the principle of God, that hath been transgressed, be lifted up; whereby the mind may be seasoned and stilled in a right understanding of the Lord, whereby his blessing enters.... For all these things happen to thee for thy good and your good, to make you to know your own strength and means, and to know the Lord's strength and power. Trust in him, therefore.

So then this is the word of the Lord God unto you all ... do not look at the temptations, confusions, corruptions, but at the light that discovers them, that makes them manifest; and with the same light you will feel over them, to receive power to stand against them. Which light discovers, the same light that lets you see sin and transgression will let you see the covenant of God, which blots out your sin and transgression, which gives victory and dominion over it, and brings into covenant with God. For looking down at sin, and corruption, and distraction, you are swallowed up in it; but looking at the light that discovers them, you will see over them.... There is the first step of peace. That will bring salvation.... So in the name and power of the Lord Jesus Christ, strengthen thee [*Journal of George Fox* (Nickalls' edition), p. 346-348].

DISCUSSION QUESTIONS:

1. What does it mean to be "still and cool" in mind and spirit?
2. Friends advise to "mind the light, not the darkness," for as Fox emphasizes, "looking down at sin, and corruption, and distraction, you are swallowed up in it, but looking at the light that discovers them.... There is the first step of peace." Discuss

more fully what this means, especially with examples for your life and the lives of others.
3. What is resonating most deeply within you?

Love silence, even in the mind; for thoughts are to that, as words to the body, troublesome; much speaking, as much thinking, spends; and in many thoughts, as well as words, there is sin. True silence is the rest of the mind, and is to the spirit what sleep is to the body, nourishment and refreshment, It is a great virtue; it covers folly, keeps secrets, avoids disputes, and prevents sin.
~ *William Penn,* Advice to His Children, *p.25.*

Section 3.J
Knowing Christ in Us

Readings: 2 Peter 1:19; *The Journal of George Fox* (John L. Nickalls, ed.), Chs. 2-3.

The Day Star. George Fox describes a confrontation with a priest:

> [The priest] took for his text these words of Peter, "We have also a more sure Word of prophecy, whereunto ye do well that ye take heed, as unto a light that shineth in a dark place, until the day dawn, and the day-star arise in your hearts." And he told the people that this was the Scriptures, by which they were to try all doctrines, religions, and opinions.
>
> Now the Lord's power was so mighty upon me, and so strong in me, that I could not hold, but was made to cry out and say, 'Oh, no; it is not the Scriptures!' and I told them what it was, namely, the Holy Spirit, by which the holy men of God gave forth the Scriptures, whereby opinions, religions, and judgments were to be tried; for it led into all truth, and so gave the knowledge of all truth. The Jews had the Scriptures, and yet resisted the Holy Ghost, and rejected Christ, the bright morning star. They persecuted Christ and His apostles, and took upon them to try their doctrines by the Scriptures; but they erred in judgment, and did not try them aright, because they tried without the Holy Ghost (Fox, p. 40).

Temples of God. Fox explained his mission to those gathered in a "steeple-house yard":

I was sent of [by] the Lord God of heaven and earth to preach freely, and to bring people off from these outward temples made with hands, which God dwelleth not in; that they might know their bodies to become the temples of God and of Christ; and to draw people off from all their superstitious ceremonies, Jewish and heathenish customs, traditions, and doctrines of men; and from all the world's hireling teachers, that take tithes and great wages, preaching for hire, and divining for money, whom God and Christ never sent, as themselves confess when they say that they never heard God's nor Christ's voice. I exhorted the people to come off from all these things, directing them to the Spirit and grace of God in themselves, and to the Light of Jesus in their own hearts; that they might come to know Christ, their free teacher, to bring them salvation, and to open the Scriptures to them. Thus the Lord gave me a good opportunity to open things largely unto them. All was quiet, and many were convinced; blessed be the Lord (Fox, pp. 87-88).

DISCUSSION QUESTIONS:

1. Friends claim that some worship the Bible, turn to the Bible, and rely on the Bible rather than worshipping, turning to, and relying on Christ. What are the consequences of relying solely on the Bible, rather than relying on Christ Jesus who opens and interprets the Bible?
2. Humanity's and our own long experience of our fallen condition means that we have a strong tendency toward error. If it is possible to get something wrong about life in the Spirit, we face fighting an ingrained tendency to do so. How do we avoid erring in our judgments and inadvertently rejecting Christ's counsel and direction?
3. What does it mean to be "sent of the Lord God?" Have you had such an experience? Please describe it.

4. What does it mean to have "become the temples of God and of Christ?"
5. What superstitions, ceremonies, customs, traditions, or doctrines have you "come off from" in turning to "the Spirit and grace of God?"
6. How do we explain knowing Christ as "free teacher" to those who say they have "never heard God's nor Christ's voice?" What about those who limit "hearing" Christ's "voice" to reading the written words of Scriptures? What about those who explain it exclusively in psychological terms?
7. What is resonating most deeply within you?

In the beginning was the Word, and the Word was with God, and the Word was God. He was with God in the beginning. Through him all things were made; without him nothing was made that has been made. In him was life, and that life was the light of men. The light shines in the darkness, but the darkness has not understood. This was the true light that gives light to every man who comes into the world.
~ John 1:1-5, 9

Chapter 4
WAITING WORSHIP

Readings: Isaiah 40:31; Matthew 18:20; John 4:23-24; Acts 1:4-5, 2:14-21; 1 Corinthians 12, 14:26-40; Robert Barclay, *Apology for the True Christian Divinity*, Prop. 11.

Christ in our midst. One persistent misunderstanding of some Friends and attenders is that Friends reject outward forms. This is not true. Friends' unique practices flow from a conviction concerning what is the right outward form. The right form for church government, worship, and ministry answers the same question: how should we act, what should be our response, if Jesus Christ is present in our midst, desiring to speak? To Friends, the answer is that we should sit in reverence, waiting for Him to speak. Thus, Friends gather in reverence, waiting to be spoken to, spoken through, and led.

When gathered with Christ Jesus who is the Head of the Church, Friends expect that there will be no speaking unless it is oracular. No one is to speak except to speak the words of God and in the power of God. The words and power of God, Friends emphasize, are perceptible as such. The words and power of God melt our hearts in an inimitable and undeniable way.

In some ways, Friends' understanding with respect to worship is closer to the "high church" liturgical traditions than the "low church" traditions of most Protestants. The highly liturgical traditions seek to center their worship on the Presence of Christ, though they often associate the Presence with the elements of their communion or Eucharist. Protestants carry on a worship program centered on a sermon surrounded with songs and prayers.

Friends intend worship to be centered on the Presence of Christ as the Living Word longing to be spoken. As the apostle Paul advised the Corinthian Church (1 Corinthians 14:26-33), anyone may share words, prayers, or songs—so long as it is as an oracle of the Spirit. There is no programmed order. Advance preparation consists of prayer and introspection, not arranging hymns and Scripture verses.

Friends have never claimed that "silence" was a consistent practice of the early church. But, if we are to speak as oracles of the Spirit, in right order, as the earliest Christians were instructed, inward stillness and outward silence *are* the first steps—until we are given what to speak and told when to speak it. Thus, we gather, not so much in silence as in submission.

Robert Barclay describes waiting worship:

> When assembled, it should be the common task of one and all to wait upon God. It should be a time for turning away from one's own thoughts and for suspending the imagination in order to feel the Presence of the Lord in the midst and to know a true gathering in his name according to his promise. Then, when everyone is thus gathered, and all meet together inwardly in their spirits, as well as outwardly in their persons, the secret power and virtue of life are known to refresh the soul. It is there that the pure motions and breathings of God's Spirit are felt to arise.

> As words of declarations, prayers, or praises arise from these promptings of the Spirit, the acceptable worship is known which edifies the church and is pleasing to God. No one limits the Spirit of God in such worship or brings forth his own laboriously assembled ideas. But everyone will state whatever the Lord has placed in his heart. And it will not be uttered from man's own will or wisdom, but in the evidence and demonstration of the Spirit and of power (p. 248).

Barclay summarizes this understanding: "Our worship consists neither in words nor in silence as such, but in a holy dependence of the mind upon God. For such dependence, it is necessary to begin with silence until the words can be brought forth which arise from God's Spirit" (p. 257-258).

Barclay claims that "even if thousands were to be convinced intellectually of the truths that we maintain, if they could not feel this inward life, and their souls did not turn away from unrighteousness, they would add nothing to us" (p. 255). He describes his own powerful experience of coming into waiting worship:

> In part, this is how I came to be a true witness. For it was not by the strength of arguments.... Rather, it was by being mysteriously reached by this life. For when I came into the silent assemblies of God's people, I felt a secret power among them, which touched my heart. And as I gave way to it, I found the evil in me weakening, and the good raised up. Thus it was that I was knit into them and united with them. And I hungered more and more for the increase of this power and life until I could feel myself perfectly redeemed (p. 254).

Friends' literature abounds with advices, descriptions, and insights concerning waiting worship, as reflected by these statements from Friends over the years, extracts published in *Quaker Faith and Practice of the Yearly Meeting of the Religious Society of Friends in Britain* (1994):

> And when God sees meet to put a Word into the mouth of any one of them [worshippers], he is to speak what the Lord hath revealed and taught him (I Cor. 2:4). So is he to give it forth in demonstration and power, and in the virtue and life of the Spirit, that it may be to edification in the church; for deep calls unto deep, and life reaches unto life, and the congregation go together to the waters to drink freely (Ps 42:7). And if anything be revealed to one that sits by, when the first is silent, that stream of the spiritual gift is turned to the other, because that spiritual liberty is in the true church,

for everyone to speak as they are moved by the Holy Spirit [Ellis Pugh (circa 1700)].

In this humanistic age, we suppose man is the initiator and God is the responder. But the living Christ within us is the initiator and we are the responders. God the Lover, the accuser, the revealer of light and darkness presses within us. "Behold, I stand at the door and knock." And all our apparent initiative is already a response, a testimonial to His secret presence and working within us. The basic response of the soul to the Light is internal adoration and joy, thanksgiving and worship, self-surrender and listening [Thomas R Kelly (1941)].

I know of no other way, in these deeper depths, of trusting in the name of the Lord, and staying upon God, than sinking into silence and nothingness before Him.... So long as the enemy can keep us reasoning, he can buffet us to and fro; but into the true solemn silence of the soul before God he cannot follow us [John Bellows (1895)].

Friends, meet together and know one another in that which is eternal, which was before the world was [George Fox (1657)].

Friends have never regarded [worship] as an individual activity. People who regard Friends' meetings as opportunities for meditation have failed to appreciate this corporate aspect. The waiting and listening are activities in which everybody is engaged and produce spoken ministry which helps to articulate the common guidance which the Holy Spirit is believed to give the group as a whole. So the waiting and listening is corporate also. This is why Friends emphasize the "ministry of silence" and the importance of coming to meeting regularly and with heart and mind prepared [John Punshon (1987)].

What is the ground and foundation of the gathered meeting? In the last analysis, it is, I am convinced, the Real Presence of God [Thomas R Kelly (1940)].

The first that enters into the place of your meeting ... turn in thy mind to the light, and wait upon God singly, as if none were present but the Lord; and here thou art strong. Then the next that comes in, let them in simplicity of heart sit down and turn in to the same light, and wait in the spirit; and so all the rest coming in, in the fear of the Lord, sit down in pure stillness and silence of all flesh, and wait in the light.... Those who are brought to a pure still waiting upon God in the spirit, are come nearer to the Lord than words are; for God is a spirit, and in the spirit is he worshipped.... In such a meeting, there will be an unwillingness to part asunder, being ready to say in yourselves, it is good to be here: and this is the end of all words and writings to bring people to the eternal living Word [Alexander Parker (1660)].

"Where two or three," says our Lord, "are gathered together in my name, there am I in the midst of them" (Mt 18:20). In these words he ... invites us not only to meet one with another but, in so doing, with himself also.... Shall the poor perishing gratifications of sense and self-love, or any inconveniences of a trivial nature, be suffered to prevent our dutiful attendance upon him, in whom alone stands our everlasting interest? Shall a cloudy sky, a little wet, a little cold, a little ease to the flesh, a view to a little earthly gain, or any common incident, furnish an excuse for declining this duty, and thereby depriving ourselves of the blessed advantage, often vouchsafed to the faithful, of enjoying heavenly communion together in spirit with the Lord of life and glory? [Yearly Meeting in London (1765)].

I went to meetings in an awful [reverent] frame of mind, and endeavored to be inwardly acquainted with the language of the true Shepherd. And one day, being under a strong exercise of spirit, I stood up, and said some words in a meeting, but not keeping close to the divine opening, I said more than was required of me and being soon sensible to my error, I was afflicted in mind some weeks, without any light or comfort, even to that degree that I could take satisfaction in nothing. I remembered God and was troubled, and in the depth of my distress he had pity upon me, and sent the Comforter. I then felt forgiveness for my offence, and my mind became calm and quiet, being truly thankful to my gracious Redeemer for his mercies. And after this, feeling the spring of divine love opened, and a concern to speak, I said a few words in a meeting in which I found peace. This I believe was about six weeks from the first time, and as I was thus humbled and disciplined under the cross, my understanding became more strengthened to distinguish the language of the pure spirit which inwardly moves upon the heart, and taught me to wait in silence sometimes many weeks together, until I felt that rise which prepares the creature to stand like a trumpet, through which the Lord speaks to his flock [John Woolman (1741)].

Ministry should be of necessity, and not of choice, and there is no living by silence, or by preaching merely [John Churchman (1734)].

The intent of all speaking is to bring into the life, and to walk in, and to possess the same, and to live in and enjoy it, and to feel God's presence [George Fox (1657)].

DISCUSSION QUESTIONS:

1. What has been your experience of the "silent assembly"?
2. What is your experience of turning away from your own thoughts and suspending your imagination?
3. How do we know if something was placed in the heart by the Lord rather than manifesting human wisdom?
4. Have you experienced the "good raised up," as Barclay did? Please explain.
5. How can we practice this "holy dependence of the mind upon God" throughout our day? Is this spiritual communion? Is this what it means to "pray without ceasing?" Are worship, spiritual communion, and prayer the same? If not, how are they related?
6. Barclay says that "One of the best things about this silent waiting upon God is that it is impossible for the enemy to counterfeit it. The devil cannot delude or deceive any soul in the exercise of it" (p. 268). Of course, a number of people can sit silently, believing they are engaging in worship even though they are not. So what did Barclay mean? What are the signs of counterfeit worship?
7. What is resonating most deeply within you?

But those who wait on the LORD shall renew their strength;
They shall mount up with wings like eagles,
They shall run and not be weary,
They shall walk and not faint.
~ Isaiah 40:31

Chapter 5
MINISTRY AND MINISTERS

Section 5.A
The Call to Ministry

Readings: Isaiah 6:1-8; *The Book of Discipline of Ohio Yearly Meeting of the Religious Society of Friends (2008)*, pgs. 30-31; *The Journal of George Fox* (John L. Nickalls, ed.), Chs. 1-2.

Isaiah 6 describes the prophet's own call to bring the word of God to His people. It is a description many Friends' ministers over the years have utilized to show what a call to ministry is like: the minister's confrontation by the Lord, the humbling recognition of how far from adequate and holy one is, the divine act of purification, and the acceptance of the call to carry a message to God's people, whatever the nature and weight of the message itself.

Who ministers? The answer to this question in a Christ-led Friends' meeting is: our Lord Jesus Christ. It is He who selects who will minister and the person selected may be man, woman, or child. It is He who gives the message that needs to be delivered to the assembled worshippers. To be a minister of our Lord is to render *free* gospel ministry, rather than serve in a hired, paid position.

Thus, in a Friends' meeting for worship, it is wrong to see the one who brings a message from the Lord as the leader of the meeting and its worship, or the center of worship. Neither the person nor the message is the center. Christ Jesus is. Nor does a Friends' minister serve in a clerical position or care for the church buildings and grounds. Friends appoint a person called the "clerk" to assemble the business agenda for monthly business meetings and that person, too, is normally not paid for the service rendered.

How are ministers made? Our Lord revealed to George Fox and other early Friends that it is not knowledge or education that fits a person for ministry. Fox relates, "As I was walking in a field on a

First-day morning, the Lord opened unto me that being bred at Oxford or Cambridge was not enough to fit and qualify men to be ministers of Christ; and I stranged [thought it strange] at it because it was the common belief of people" [*Journal*, Nickalls edition, 7]. Ministers are made by God, not man. Self-styled prophets need not apply. The most members of a meeting can do is recognize a special gift for ministry our Lord has given to particular individuals, who are scrupulously obedient to the Lord's leading and serve Him and them humbly, faithfully, and in holiness.

As our Lord forms His ministers to function well in His service, He may challenge them in numerous ways, something George Fox's own experience well illustrates. George Fox wrote in his *Journal*:

> I went back into Nottinghamshire, and there the Lord showed me that the natures of those things which were hurtful without [outwardly] were within, in the hearts and minds of wicked men. The natures of dogs, swine, vipers, of Sodom and Egypt, Pharaoh, Cain, Ishmael, Esau, etc. The natures of these I saw within, though people had been looking without. I cried to the Lord, saying, "Why should I be thus, seeing I was never addicted to commit those evils?" And the Lord answered that it was needful I should have a sense of all conditions, how else should I speak to all conditions; and in this I saw the infinite love of God (p. 19).

Among the conditions George Fox experienced is one common to us all, the temptation to doubt:

> One morning, as I was sitting by the fire, a great cloud came over me, and a temptation beset me; but I sat still. And it was said, "All things come by nature"; and the elements and stars came over me, so that I was in a manner quite clouded with it. But insomuch I sat, still and silent, the people of the house

perceived nothing. And as I sat still under it and let it alone, a living hope arose in me, and a true voice, which said, "There is a living God who made all things." And immediately the cloud and temptation vanished away, and life rose over it all, and my heart was glad, and I praised the living God.

After some time, I met with some people who had a notion that there was no God but that all things came by nature and I had a great dispute with them and overturned them, and made some of them confess that there *was* a living God. Then I saw that it was good that I had gone through that exercise. And we had great meetings in those parts, for the power of the Lord broke through in that side of the country (p. 25).

DISCUSSION QUESTIONS:

1. Identify other differences you see between a Christ-led Friends minister and the position of minister, pastor, evangelist, or priest in other Christian bodies.
2. How does the passage in 1 Corinthians 14:32-33 ("The spirits of the prophets are subject to the control of the prophets. For God is not a God of disorder, but of peace.") reflect Friends' understanding of ministry and its discipline?
3. Fox writes that those things that are outwardly hurtful are inwardly part of our hearts and minds. He describes these things as the "natures" of vipers, Sodom, Egypt, Cain, etc. Can you identify what kinds of natures or characters Fox is identifying with this language?
4. Some Christians believe they should be able to speak to all conditions, like Fox and Paul, but what are the grave pitfalls in having such an attitude? Why were both Fox and Paul able to avoid such deadly pitfalls?
5. Discuss the wisdom of sitting still under a temptation to doubt, rather than struggling against it or trying to flee from it?

6. Why is it important to see our doubts and temptations in the larger context of our lives and God's work, rather than as simply discrete events unrelated to other experiences and challenges?
7. What resonates most deeply within you?

Heed not distressing thoughts when they rise ever so strongly in thee; fear them not, but be still awhile, not believing in the power which thou feels they have over thee, and it will fall on a sudden. It is good for thy spirit and greatly to thy advantage to be much and variously exercised by the Lord. Thou dost not know what the Lord hath already done and what he is yet doing for thee therein.
~ Isaac Pennington

Section 5.B
Women Ministers

Readings: Margaret Fell, "Chapter 3: Women's Speaking Justified," *A Sincere and Constant Love: An Introduction to the Work of Margaret Fell.* Edited with Introductions by T.H.S. Wallace. Richmond, IN: Friends United Press, 2009.

Quakers, from their beginning, recognized God's public call of women to a ministry equal to that of men, as an essential part of the New Covenant. This acceptance of women as spiritual equals had nothing to do with a social or political agenda to liberate women, nor was it because of cultural progress or change. In fact, the social and political agendas of the time and the culture were opposed to women's ministry. Early Friends, however, emphasized the inclusiveness of the New Covenant, explicit for gender in the prophecy of Joel 2:28-32 and repeated in Acts 2:17-18, in which God declares "I will pour out my Spirit on all people. Your sons and daughters will prophesy, your young men will see visions, your old men will dream dreams. Even on my servants, both men and women, I will pour out my Spirit in those days and they will prophesy." In keeping with that prophecy, as our Lord's Spirit poured upon women of the first Quaker generation, they were in the forefront of the work of declaring the gospel and suffering for it. Women were often the first Quaker ministers to appear in new fields, including in the West Indies, Barbados, and the early American colonies. Women were also among the first Quaker martyrs.

Margaret Fell, an influential leader of the first Quaker generation, wrote a tightly ordered argument for women's ministry in her pamphlet *Women's Speaking Justified,* reviewing in detail the doctrinal and scriptural bases for women's spiritual equality in

Christ. As Terry Wallace notes in his *Introduction to the Work of Margaret Fell*:

> Fell reviews the special favor God has shown the female sex through redemptive history: that God calls His church by the name of woman, both in the Old and New Testaments, and that by woman His Son entered the world. Further, Fell notes the special regard of Christ for women, including the woman of Samaria, Mary and Martha, Mary Magdalene, and Mary the mother of James. Not only are women received openly and treated as spiritual equals with men, but they also play primary roles in Jesus' resurrection and the proclamation of the gospel. They are the first at the Tomb. They are sent to the disciples to tell them the Good News. Mary Magdalene, herself, is the first to witness Christ risen.... [Fell] soundly puts away the objections of those who would silence women as the weaker sex, not by arguing women's strength, but by slaying the weaker sex argument with a Christian one: "The weakness of God is stronger than men" (p. 95-96).

Fell did not argue on the basis of culture against Paul's declaration (in 1 Corinthians and 1 Timothy) that women must keep silent in the churches. Instead, Fell disposed of it in two other ways. First, she reviewed the verses in the fuller Pauline context, citing many of Paul's other references to women working and ministering in the church. In that review, Fell effectively demonstrated that Paul had no problem with *holy* women speaking, women who labored with him in the gospel. Second, Fell emphasized that the Pauline strictures are not against all women, but only against those yet in the Fall, unresponsive to God's Spirit. Women without Christ's Spirit remain under the Law, and the Law indeed bans them from speaking. However, women of the New Covenant were another matter. To stop their mouths was to stop Christ Himself from speaking!

Speaking the words of God in the power of God is essential to worshipping and governing the Church in Spirit and Truth. Both men and women are expected by Friends to be used by God in that work. The New Covenant understanding of women's spiritual equality, grasped by Quakers from the beginning, remains deeply relevant today as the majority of Christendom has yet to come to terms with women's position in Christ's ministry and kingdom.

DISCUSSION QUESTIONS:

1. Do you feel comfortable with having women minister in meeting for worship?
2. What has been your experience of women's ministry?
3. Does the evidence of women ministering in the New Testament impress you?

Section 5.C
Speaking during Worship

Readings: 1 Corinthians 2:3-5, 13:2, 14:1-5, 22-33, 39; 1 Peter 4:10-11; Lewis Benson, "On Being Moved By the Spirit to Minister in Public Worship" in *The Quaker Vision*; Ruth Pitman, *On the Vocal Ministry*; Thomas Gould, *The Inspired Ministry*: Charles Marshall, "An Epistle to Friends Coming Forth in the Ministry."

Pursue Love, desire to prophesy (1 Cor. 14: 1). Eventually, almost everyone who worships with Friends will wonder, *Am I to speak?* And, again, eventually, almost everyone will doubt that someone who spoke should have.

Learning how to speak during worship is a recurring theme in the journals of Friends. Those who spoke too soon, too late, too long, too little, or with the wrong words report an uncomfortable inward correction afterwards, just as those who failed to speak at all do. Conservative Friends take quite seriously the scriptural injunction to those gifted with words to speak to do so only as an "oracle of God." It is the fundamental basis of our ministry during worship.

But we must not be paralyzed by the prospect of speaking. So long as our deep desire is to serve God, and we are not trying to impress others, then we can rely on two questions in helping us decide to speak. The first is, Has Christ given me a message for all of us—or only for myself? The second is, Is Christ prompting me to share that message at this very moment?

If there is any doubt, the usual advice is to remain quietly in prayer. Since the Lord may be dealing directly with others during the silence, it is best not to interrupt what may be going on within them, unless it is clear you should do so. Sometimes Friends decide they got it wrong—they start to speak, then feel they should not, in which event the unquestioned advice is to sit back down and be quiet. Messages are never given in response to another, and it is highly unusual for a Friend to speak more than once in one meeting for worship.

Some Friends may experience a clear command to speak immediately even though the words have not been given. These Friends usually stand and await the words. Other Friends may feel the call to stand about the time that an outline of the message is given. Still others may sense the call when the first few words are given. Or others may know the entire message and simply wait until the call comes to speak it at a particular moment. Sometimes Friends report an exceptional and unusual quickening of the heart (not merely "butterflies" or common anxiety in public speaking), or a sense of looming regret if the message is not immediately delivered. Sometimes the message may be sung or prayed. Some Friends report an indescribable sense of release, if faithful. Ultimately, each of us must rely on Christ to teach us directly how to do His bidding.

When others speak, we should be prayerful, asking the Lord what He would have us hear. Sometimes, we will hear nothing that resonates within us. In such events, we should prayerfully let go of what is said and not analyze or dissect it afterwards. Sometimes, we will hear the Lord's words convicting us or comforting us. If this is the case, we should not attribute the words to the speaker but directly to Christ. We should let the Holy Spirit work. If we are so inclined, we may afterwards let the speaker know how the message affected us so that the speaker's decision to speak can be confirmed.

Sometimes we hear only the voice of a person in need. And, in these cases especially, we should ask the Lord what we need to hear. Sometimes, the need is a simple need to share a joy or concern that is pressing on the speaker. Other times, the need may be something more substantial or even disturbing. Regardless, the right response is prayer. These prayers can transform the situation in the moment, or show us something we can do or say afterwards to help the speaker.

When considering whether or not to speak during worship, and when listening to others speak, we should always remember George

Fox's advice: "Friends, be careful how ye set your feet among the tender plants that are springing up out of God's earth; lest ye tread upon them, hurt, bruise, or crush them in God's vineyard."

Wait and watch. Charles Marshall's epistle gives advice for offering vocal ministry:

> Dearly beloved Friends, Who in your assemblies sometimes feel a testimony for the Lord to spring to your hearts, keep your watch in the light, so that none stay behind, nor run before; but let all that open their mouths in the assemblies of the Lord's people, do it as the oracle of God, in the arising of the eternal power; for nothing can beget to God, but what comes from the word of life, that lives and abides forever; and nothing can refresh, strengthen or comfort that which is begotten by the word of life, but what springs from the same. Therefore, dear Friends, whom this concerns, wait diligently, not only to know and savor every motion, but also to know the appointed time when the motion should be brought forth ... where there is not a waiting for the perfecting of what is to be brought forth, but instead thereof, coming forth before the time, there is an untimely birth; which hurts the vessel through which it comes, and the hearers are burdened; and the life which first moved comes to be oppressed....

> Friends, this lies upon my spirit to all who feel the beginning of a testimony spring in your hearts, wait diligently in that light, low, in stillness and passiveness of spirit, and you will come to feel the counsel of the Lord sealed to your understandings, and see the time when to speak, and when to remain silent, and here will be a right increase of your testimony. When that which is sealed to the understanding is offered, retire inward and sink down into stillness, and keep in the valley; and let all know that no ministration, save that

which comes from the life itself, from the fresh arising of the pure power of the Lord, avails anything; and all ministering out of this will fade and come to an end, in the approaching day of trial....

And, Friends, when any through want of experience err, in running before the power, be very tender....

DISCUSSION QUESTIONS:

1. Have you been raised up by God's power to speak a message from Him? What has been your experience in responding to His motion?
2. What has been your experience of speaking during worship?
3. Have you resisted a message presented to you to give? What was your experience of "judgment" for failing the Lord's call?
4. Have you experienced a stop in mid-message and obeyed it? What transpired thereafter?
5. Have you been strongly reached by some particular message spoken by another during worship? Please explain its impact.
6. Why is it important for a spoken message to come from God?
7. Marshall distinguishes between being given the message and delivering the message at exactly the right moment. Why can timing be important? Is there always a single right moment for a message to be spoken?
8. What has been your experience of being "spoken to" by God through a person's message outside of meeting for worship?
9. What is the important function of silent waiting worship (instead of a worship program) for the speaker(s)? What is the important function of silent waiting worship for those who listen to the speaker?
10. What is resonating most deeply within you?

If anyone speaks, he should do it as one speaking the very words of God. If anyone serves, he should do it with the strength God provides, so that in all things God may be praised through Jesus Christ. To him be the glory and the power for ever and ever. Amen.
~ *1 Peter 4:11*

Section 5.D
Advice to Ministers

Readings: Samuel Bownas, "To the Meetings of the Ministers at Kendal in Westmoreland."

Counsel and caution. The following was written by Samuel Bownas in 1702:

> My dearly beloved Brethren and Sisters, in that love which in time past we have enjoyed together, do I heartily salute you, having in mind some few things to impart, as counsel and caution to us all, including myself therein.
>
> We who apprehend ourselves called into this public station of preaching ought closely to wait on our Guide to put us forth in the work. And dear friends, I see great need for us to carefully mind our openings, and go on as we are led by the Spirit; for if we overrun our Guide and opening we shall be confused, not knowing where, or how to conclude. But if we begin and go on with the Spirit, we shall conclude so that all who are truly spiritual will sensibly feel that we are right. Thus will our ministry edify them that hear it.
>
> And dear friends, let us be singly and in sincerity devoted to the will of God, whether to preach or be silent; for if we are not sensible of such a resignation, it is doubtful that we may set ourselves at work, when we should be quiet, and so bring an uneasiness upon our friends, and burthen upon ourselves. And this conduct will shut up Friends' hearts against our service and ministry. And my dear friends, every time you appear in the ministry, when it is over, examine yourselves narrowly, whether you have kept in your places, and to your

Guide; and consider whether you have not used superfluous words that render the matter disagreeable, or such tones or gestures as mis-become the work we are about, always remembering that the true ministers preach not themselves, but Christ Jesus our Lord. Let us bear this in mind that neither arts, strength of memory, nor former experiences will, without the sanctification of the spirit, do anything for us to depend on. Let us therefore, I entreat you, keep to the living fountain, the spring of eternal life, opened by our Lord Jesus Christ in our hearts.

I also desire, that you would not neglect your day's work, in visiting the dark corners of the counties about you; but be mindful of your service therein, as the Lord shall make way for it.

The things above written have been on my mind to communicate to you, my dear friends, with desires that the God and Father of our Lord Jesus Christ may be with your spirits, Amen. Hoping, also, that I shall not be forgotten by you, in your nearest supplications to the God of the spirits of all flesh; remembering me, that I may be preserved by sea, and in the wilderness, through the many and various exercises and baptisms that I may be suffered to undergo for the services' sake; and that I may be preserved in humility and self-denial, under the power of the cross, the most beautiful ornaments a minister can ever be clothed with; that if it please Him we should meet again, and our joy may then be full in the Holy Ghost, which is the fervent prayer of your exercised friend and brother, SAMUEL BOWNAS.

DISCUSSION QUESTIONS:

1. Early Friends understood those called into the "public station of preaching" to be subject to additional burdens of being prepared

inwardly and outwardly, living a rightly-ordered life (being "clothed with" humility and self-denial). How do we keep ourselves prepared to be ministered through? How does a disorderly life affect our usefulness?
2. In practical terms, how do we examine ourselves to know we have kept to our place and sought our Guide Jesus Christ when speaking in worship?
3. What is resonating most deeply within you?

Section 5.E
The Traveling Ministry and Visiting Families

Readings: George Fox, *The Journal of George Fox*, Nickalls edition, p. 34-36; Samuel Bownas, *A Description of the Qualifications Necessary to a Gospel Minister: Advice to Ministers and Elders Among the People Called Quakers.*

The beginning of the traveling ministry and visitation among Quakers coincided with the rise of the Quakers themselves. Early Quaker ministers and leaders—both men and women—traveled throughout England, Ireland, Europe, and the American colonies, carrying the good news that Jesus Christ was present and powerful to save people not only in their sin, but from that sin. This ministry included addressing large open-air gatherings, worshipping and ministering in established Friends' meetings, and making spiritual visits to Quaker families, no matter how scattered they were across the world. Friends' ministers traveled under the prompting and direction of the Holy Spirit for the purposes of declaring the gospel and building up Friends in the faith.

It should be understood that what passes for "visitation" today among most Friends has little to do with the traveling ministry and spiritual visitation described here. Visiting among Friends in the twentieth and twenty-first centuries has often become little more that shallow socializing, during which weighty spiritual topics and personal spiritual concerns are rarely discussed. A second, more serious purpose of this latter-day visiting is for "conflict resolution" in troubled meetings or the presentation of some personal or political concern.

Testing a prompting to travel: Before the twentieth century, when Friends began to experience promptings to travel on a spiritual concern, they normally sought counsel and advice from others—

especially the elders and overseers in their meeting, first for the purpose of testing a leading (Was it a prompting from Christ Jesus? From one's own pride and ego? Or worst of all, from the Enemy?). Faithful ministers were careful not to "run before their Guide," and the testing of a leading often took many weeks or months, in some cases years. The inclusion of the meeting community in the minister's seeking of clearness was of key importance, because of the Quaker commitment to "free gospel ministry." Quaker ministers were not paid, and to travel in ministry was time-consuming and a major sacrifice for ministers and their families. The inclusion of the meeting meant that when one's fellow Friends united that a particular leading was truly from Christ Jesus, they took it as a spiritual responsibility to see that the minister's family and livelihood would be cared for and maintained. This was more than simply an added labor for the meeting. Given the vicissitudes of travel in past centuries, there was the possibility that ministers might die during their journeys. Many early Friends ministers were injured and jailed, and some died in prison in the seventeenth century. Mary Dyer was hung with three other Friends by New England Puritans for bringing them the gospel. Elizabeth Hooten died in Barbados after intrepid ministry that took her thousands of miles from her home in the North of England. In the eighteenth century, John Woolman died of smallpox in England during his travel in ministry. Such sacrifice was not only weighty for the individual minister, but also for the family and the meeting, and the meeting's support of its minister(s) was taken with great seriousness.

Seeking a traveling companion or companions: Young Friends ministers often received valuable spiritual experience in the traveling ministry and spiritual visitation when they were prompted by the Spirit and selected by their meeting to accompany a seasoned, older, and far more experienced minister. Present-day readers should be careful to understand that such arrangements were *not* what today we would characterize as an *internship* or *mentoring*. Having a traveling companion, young or old, could be a particular blessing, for the minister had a partner in prayer, an adviser with whom the minister could seek spiritual counsel and check perceptions, a companion who could both exhort and admonish as need be. The elders and overseers of a visited meeting would occasionally also help in this work, providing an extra check the minister could call upon as needed. One minister was raised up in the Spirit to speak to a "wolfish" spirit in a meeting he was visiting. Having not observed the presence of such a person or attitude, he was very concerned he might have perceived in error the prompting to speak. Asking for time with the elders of that meeting to present his concern—and if necessary, confess he was amiss, if that proved to be the fact—he was told that indeed his ministry was spot on and had addressed a problem with which the meeting had long suffered. The individual with the wolfish spirit, the minister was told, had been reached by the divine rebuke, had repented of his troubling attitude, and had begun to seek forgiveness of Friends.

Examples from the history of Friends' ministry: Traveling ministry was often physically arduous, spiritually difficult, and at times dangerous. Friends' journals are filled with notes on the distances traveled and under what conditions, as well as the situations they discovered and had to address when they reached their destinations. One Friends minister records having to travel twenty miles in up-state New York, breaking his way through chest high snow drifts only to arrive at a distant Quaker family's cabin where he had to sleep in the loft of the building with snow sifting through the shingles all night long.

Traveling ministry could also be spiritually trying – and dangerous if one got off one's watch. Some ministers experienced a spiritual emptying in preparation for visiting families. John Woolman reports:

Traveling up and down of late, I have had renewed evidences that to be faithful to the Lord, and content with his will concerning me, is a most useful lesson to be learning, looking less at the effect of my labor than at the pure motion and reality of the concern, as it arises from heavenly love. In the Lord Jehovah is everlasting strength; and as the mind in humble resignation is united to him, and we utter words from an inward knowledge that they arise from the heavenly spring, though our way may be difficult, and it may require close watch to keep in it, and though the matter into which we may be led may tend to our own abasement; yet, if we continue in patience and meekness, heavenly peace will be the reward of our labors (*Journal of John Woolman*, edited by Charles Eliot, 1909, p. 222).

Being emptied spiritually was often necessary so one could deliver what the Lord required, not giving advice in one's own wisdom or seeking an outcome that one considered appropriate. For instance, one was not entering a situation as an expert problem solver, but as a disciple of Christ Jesus. One minister, being asked by a Friend involved in a bitter and long-running feud with his Quaker neighbor over a disputed water course between their property, was not given instructions on how to resolve the conflict (indeed, many Friends and committees had already tried). The minister simply received the words from the Spirit: "More is expected of some than others." That statement proved to be the seed that grew in the hearer until he became convinced he had to go to his irascible neighbor and wash his feet, an act that changed the entire situation (though his neighbor was at first resistant) and led to the end of the conflict. Traveling in faith to bring a word from one's Lord required extraordinary openness to His Holy Spirit.

DISCUSSION QUESTIONS:

1. Have you ever felt promptings to travel in ministry? What form did this take? Did those promptings fade or carry you forward to do Christ's work?
2. In the presence of such promptings, did you seek clearness with others as to whether the promptings were indeed valid spiritual promptings? What form did this clearness seeking take? What was the outcome?
3. If you have traveled in ministry with a companion or companions, what was particularly positive in that companionship? Were there missteps your spiritual companion(s) helped you to avoid? Identify one or two of these, for which you are thankful.
4. Have you experienced any bitter moments in ministry, during which you felt you spoke in your own power, not at the Spirit's prompting? What were the results? Did you receive some "sense of correction" from the Lord? What forms did this correction take?
5. Why must the prayer "Lord, your will be done," be the touchstone of the ministry, local or traveling? What have you seen happen when our Lord's will is not sought in ministry? What have you seen happen when it is sought?

*I was early convinced in my mind that true religion consisted in an inward life wherein the heart doth love and reverence God the Creator and learns to exercise true justice and goodness not only toward all men but also toward the brute creation; that as the mind was moved on an inward principle to love God as an invisible, incomprehensible being, on the same principle it was moved to love him in all his manifestations in the visible world; that as by his breath the flame of life was kindled in all animal and sensitive creatures, to say we love God ... and at the same time exercise cruelty toward the least creature ...
was a contradiction in itself.
~ John Woolman*

Section 5.F
Examples of the Nature of Ministry from Quaker History

Readings: Thomas B. Gould, *The Inspired Ministry*.

Example 1: James Scribbens

When the gift preaches. Thomas Gould reports that James Scribbens was:

> A man of very small natural talents indeed, not having common sense or being capable of procuring his own livelihood, or even of knowing when he had eaten or drunken sufficiently; but he had a very striking, convincing, and remarkable gift in the ministry conferred upon him, under the exercise of which it was no unusual occurrence for him to bring tears from the eyes of the audience, to such a degree that there would be wet spots upon the floor between the benches on which the people sat.

> On his first rising, his appearance was so contemptible, and his manner so incoherent, and sometimes so nonsensical that it produced laughter among those who were assembled. But the old man would pull the cap which he wore upon his head, one way and another, and say to such as made themselves merry, "My good Master has not come yet. When He does come, you will laugh on the other side of your mouths!" which was generally verified, as the Life and Power arose into dominion; the excellency of the Power being rendered more fully apparent by the manifest weakness of the instrument made use of, that no flesh should glory in the Master's presence.

After James had been powerfully engaged in testimony in the large public meetings during yearly meeting week, on returning to his lodgings, before a room full of company, he boasted that he preached, and that he preached excellently, too.

"No, James," said Mary Richardson, "thou art greatly mistaken; thou hast not preached this day."

Why, he was sure he had, and that he did it well.

"No, James, it was thy gift that preached," said Mary Richardson.

James Scribbens belonged to South Kingston Monthly Meeting, and lived sometimes with one Friend, and sometimes with another, in different parts of the Narragansett Country. He was usually employed in some way which did not require much skill or thought; and at one time, while residing in the family of a Friend who lived near to one Doctor MacSparran [an episcopal priest], and being engaged in repairing a breach in a stone wall by the roadside, the doctor, who entertained a most contemptible opinion of the Quakers in general, and of James Scribbens in particular, in passing by on horseback, reined up his horse, and thus accosted him:

"Well, James, how many tons of pudding and milk will it take to make forty rods of stone wall?"

James dropped the stone which he held in his hand, and looking at the self-sufficient doctor, said, "Just as many as it will take of hireling priests to make a Gospel minister!"

It so happened that a man of note and learning attended a meeting in which James Scribbens preached; and was so affected by what he heard that at the close of the meeting, he requested some Friend with whom he was acquainted to introduce him to the speaker, commending the sermon in strong terms, and remarking that so great a preacher must be a very sensible and learned man, and that he wished to have some religious conversation with him and to ask him some questions.

The Friend endeavored to divert him from his purpose, by explaining the nature of our principles with regard to the ministry; that it was neither natural nor acquired abilities, but the reception of a heavenly gift, and the renewed extension of Divine favor, which rendered the labors of our ministers so weighty and powerful; that they were not however always alike favored; that this gift was sometimes bestowed in a remarkable manner, not only upon illiterate men, but upon those of small natural understanding; so that if he were introduced to such in private, after witnessing their public services, he would be at once surprised and disappointed.

It was difficult to put the inquirer by [and after several such meetings] the Friend could no longer resist. He accordingly introduced the parties to each other at another Friend's house; but the man whose feelings had been so wrought upon, and whose expectations had been raised to such a height, manifested his surprise and disappointment, upon attempting to enter into religious conversation with [him], by exclaiming to the Friend who had done his best to prevent it, "He is a fool!"—and instead of putting difficult theological questions to this weak but sometimes highly favored instrument, for solution, he simply asked him the meaning of some ordinary words in the English language; to which James, with great simplicity, replied that he did not know.

"But," said the inquirer, "you made use of those words in your preaching today."

"Very well," said James Scribbens, "I knew then!"

In the conclusion, this man confessed that he had read many books upon the subject, but that his acquaintance with James Scribbens had furnished the most conclusive evidence of the truth of the Quaker doctrine of divine immediate revelation that he had ever met with.

Example 2: Isaac Lawton and A Servant Boy

A work of the Spirit, not the intellect. According to Thomas B. Gould:

> During the war of the Revolution, the British army took possession of Rhode Island and kept it for some time—I think one or two years. A company of these troops was stationed in the Friends' meeting house at Portsmouth. One day, while Friends were thus deprived of the use of it, Isaac Lawton, a minister in good esteem who belonged to that meeting, felt his mind drawn to go to the meeting house, from which he lived about two miles distant. He went, and after some time, commenced preaching to the soldiers present. The opening on his mind was large, the concern weighty, and he expected to have much to say; but he had not proceeded far, when his way seemed entirely closed; he felt a full stop, and sat down abruptly. This surprised him, after so large an opening, and having, as he thought, clearly seen how he was to treat the subject.

He had, however, scarcely taken his seat, when a little negro boy (I think about twelve years of age), who was present in attendance upon one of the officers, stood up with the same subject, commencing where Isaac had left off, and treating it as he had expected to do. He went on with such clearness and authority, and kept so close to what had been opened to Isaac's view, that the latter fully expected to be released from further labor on that occasion. But the little boy, after having spoken at some length, sat down as suddenly and unexpectedly to Isaac, as his appearance had been unexpected and striking.

Isaac Lawton took up the subject where the boy left it, and continued to speak until he had relieved his own mind.

DISCUSSION QUESTIONS:

1. What in these anecdotes strikes you?
2. Have you ever experienced anything similar to either of these instances?
3. What is resonating most deeply within you?

Chapter 6
CHRIST'S PEOPLE: THE CHURCH VISIBLE AND INVISIBLE

Section 6.A
Christ's People

Readings: Matthew 11:27; John 14:6 and 26; John 15; Acts 2:16-17; Romans 8:9, 8:14-17; Galatians 1:15-17, 3:27, 5:21-25; Colossians 1:27; 1 Corinthians 2:9-10, 5:9-12, 12; 2 Corinthians 13:5;1 John 1:5-7; Robert Barclay, *Apology for the True Christian Divinity*,Prop. 2, § III – VI, X (Freiday).

Christians have the Spirit of Christ. Barclay says that although Jesus is no longer with us in His flesh, He teaches and instructs us inwardly through His Spirit, and that the only means of knowing God is the revelation of God through Jesus' leading us. Barclay understands this as the essence of Christianity:

> Christianity has become, as it were, an art, acquired by human knowledge and industry, like any other art or science. Men have not only assumed the name of Christians by certain artificial tricks, but they have even procured the honor for themselves of being considered masters of Christianity, even though they are altogether strangers to the spirit and life of Jesus. But if we make a definition of a Christian which is scriptural, that a Christian is one who has the Spirit of Christ and is led by it, we will have to divest many [so-called] Christians ... of that designation.
>
> When Christians are learned in all other methods of obtaining knowledge—whether it be the letter of the Scriptures, the traditions of the churches, or the works of creation and providence—and are able to produce strong and undeniable arguments from these sources, but remain altogether ignorant of the inward and unmediated revelations

of God's Spirit in the heart, they ought not be considered Christians (p. 22).

Take away the Spirit and Christianity is no more Christianity than a corpse is a man, once the soul and spirit have departed. And a corpse is a noisome and a useless thing which the living can no longer stand and bury out of sight, no matter how acceptable it was when it was actuated and moved by the soul (p. 32).

DISCUSSION QUESTIONS:

1. If someone confidently considers himself to be a Christian because of his knowledge of the Scriptures, but he is a stranger to the spirit and life of Jesus, what are the consequences—to him and to others?
2. When do we have a spiritual duty to tell someone he or she seems to be a stranger to the spirit of Jesus, even though he or she loudly claims to be a Christian?
3. What are the differences between being a "seeker" of Jesus and being a "finder"?
4. Is there an appropriate role for the "other methods" of obtaining knowledge? How do we know when we are pursuing such knowledge under the Holy Spirit's guidance?

Section 6.B
The Church Visible and Invisible

Readings: Robert Barclay, *Apology for the True Christian Divinity*, Prop. X (Freiday).

The world in which the Quakers appeared in the seventeenth century was, like twenty-first century North America, populated by numerous sects, more than a few vying for the religious and secular title of the "one true church." Faced with this confusing mixed multitude of religious bodies and competing churches, early Friends distinguished the true Church from the false churches. The latter were easy to identify, as Jesus had said (Matthew 7:20), by the fruits they bore. Those churches preached a false gospel, persecuted faithful people, and ran after power and wealth. As Robert Barclay explains below, Friends saw the true Church as represented by two overlapping groups of faithful souls: the invisible Church and the visible.

The true Church invisible. Robert Barclay described the invisible Church (i.e., fully visible only to God):

> [This is the] company of those whom God has called out of the world and the worldly spirit, to walk in his light and life.... It includes both those who are still in this inferior world and those who, having already laid down the earthly tabernacle, have passed into their heavenly mansions.... [Although some] may be outwardly unknown to and distant from those who profess Christ and Christianity in words and have the benefit of the Scriptures, yet they have become sanctified by their obedience and cleansed from the evil of their ways.... There may be members of this catholic Church not only among all the several sorts of Christians, but also

among pagans, Turks, and Jews.... They may be blind in their understanding of some things, and perhaps burdened with the superstitions and ceremonies of [their] sects ... [but] they are upright in their hearts before the Lord, aiming and endeavoring to be delivered from iniquity, and loving to follow righteousness... (p. 172-173).

Since the Spirit of Christ is universally bestowed but the "benefit of the Scriptures" has not been, it follows that there are those who have been "sanctified by their obedience and cleansed from their evil ways," having responded to God's promptings, even without knowing the Scriptures. Barclay considers those who do not have the Scriptures to be sometimes somewhat blind in their understandings, but he believes God is willing to be reconciled with everyone "aiming and endeavoring to be delivered from iniquity, and loving to follow righteousness."

Barclay is clear that the universal possibility of reconciliation with God "does not do away with the absolute necessity for believing the outward testimony where God has afforded the opportunity for knowing it." He explains that the "testimony of the Spirit as recorded in the Scriptures answers the testimony of the same Spirit in the heart." Thus, those truly moved by the Holy Spirit will recognize the authorship of the Scriptures and believe their testimony.

The true Church visible. The Church that is visible not only to God but also to the suffering world is the local "fellowship" of those who have been "brought to a belief in the true principles and doctrines of the Christian faith." To be a member of this kind of fellowship, "not only is [the] inward work indispensably necessary, but also profession of belief in Jesus Christ and in the holy truths delivered by his Spirit in the Scriptures." Barclay describes the visible local fellowships of Christians: "With their hearts united by the same love, and their understanding informed by the same truths, they gather, meet, and assemble together to wait upon God, to worship him, and to bear a joint testimony for the truth against error and to suffer for this truth. Through this fellowship, they become in many respects like one family and household. They watch over, instruct, and care for one another according to their several abilities and attainments" (p. 174).

The visible fellowships of Christians have the benefit of Scripture and the love of one another. With their "understandings informed" and their mutual care, they are not blind in their understandings, burdened with superstitions, or deprived of true spiritual community. They are, thus, better prepared to endure the "inward work" and to bear a "joint testimony for the truth" of the Church. On the one hand, this description of the Church is very expansive. Anyone, regardless of initial religious understanding, may be brought into the universal Church. But, on the other hand, this description of the Church is very restrictive. To be brought into the Church, one must be "sanctified" by actual obedience.

Early Friends did not underestimate how difficult it was to be part of the Church by being "sanctified by obedience." Their writings record their deep struggles for obedience. Being freed from the burdens of blind understandings and superstitions, and being given the care and support of others seeking sanctification by obedience, was a tremendous assistance. It was Christian duty to provide this assistance, and thus Friends were motivated to endure tremendous persecution in order to bring Jews, Muslims, Native Americans, Roman Catholics, and Protestants into visible fellowship with Friends. This evangelization was part of Friends' "joint testimony for the truth."

DISCUSSION QUESTIONS:

1. Barclay described mistaken religious understandings as a burden to following Christ and the Scriptures and fellowship of

Christians as a benefit. Is the burden/benefit concept helpful? In what ways do you find it so?
2. Membership in the Church for early Friends meant "sanctification by obedience"—forsaking evil and being reconciled to God. This is not a mere matter of good intentions and hopes. It is a matter of responding to what has been required. More is required of some than of others because greater measures of the Spirit are given to some than to others. Why does this standard of actual obedience offend our contemporary sensibilities?
3. What does it mean to be part of "a joint testimony for truth"? What does that testimony require of God's gathered people?
4. What about those who have never heard an accurate outward testimony but rather only a garbled and mistaken interpretation of Christianity and the Scriptures? Are those who forsake the churches of mistaken Christianity—"spiritual refugees"—in a similar situation to those to whom true Christianity has never been made available?
5. What is resonating most deeply within you?

Children, Fear God; that is to say, have an holy awe upon your minds to avoid that which is evil, and a strict care to embrace and do that which is good. The measure and standard of which knowledge and duty is the light of Christ in your consciences, by which, as in John 3: 20, 21, you may clearly see if your deeds—aye, and your words and thoughts, too, are wrought in God or not (for they are the deeds of the mind, and for which you must be judged); I say, with this divine light of Christ in your consciences, you may bring your thoughts, words, and works to judgment in yourselves, and have a right, true, sound, and unerring sense of your duty towards God and man. And as you come to obey this blessed light in its holy convictions, it will lead you out of the world's dark and degenerate ways and works, and bring you unto Christ's way and life, and to be of the number of his true, self-denying followers, to take up your cross for his sake, that bore his for yours, and to become the children of the Light, putting it on as your Holy armor, by which you may see and resist the fiery darts of Satan's temptations, and overcome him in all his assaults.
~ *William Penn*, Advices to His Children, Ch.I.2, pp.4-5

Fear God; show it in desire, refraining and doing; keep the inward watch, keep a clear soul and a light heart. Mind an inward sense upon doing anything. When you read the Scripture, remark the notablest places, as your spirits are most touched and affected, in a common-place book, with that sense or opening which you receive; for they come not by study or in the will of man, no more than the Scripture did; and they may be lost by carelessness and overgrowing thoughts, and businesses of this life; so in perusing any other good or profitable book, yet rather meditate than read much. For the spirit of a man knows the things of a man, and with that spirit, by observation of the tempers and, actions of men you see in the world, and looking into your own spirits, and meditating thereupon, you will have a deep and strong judgment of men and things. For from what may be, what should be, and what is most probable or likely to be, you can hardly miss in your judgment of human affairs; and you have a better spirit than your own in reserve for a time of need, to pass the final judgment in important matters.
~ *William Penn,* Advices to His Children, Ch.II.2, pp.18-99

Section 6.C
The Place of the Individual in the Body of Christ

Reading: William Penn, *True Spiritual Liberty*

Western individualism, which elevates individuals above the group, destroys community, eats away at our concern for others' welfare, and too often produces cadres of self-styled prophets who point the way to promised lands in their own imaginations. However, there are many religious bodies who expect complete obedience to the group and its leaders, obedience enforced with expulsion, excommunication, shunning, or other more draconian devices.

Perhaps because the first Quakers saw around them so many examples of both rampant individualism—like the Ranters of their day—and oppressive religious and political bodies, they recognized that the question of individual versus group discernment is a critical one. What happens when an individual's discernment conflicts with that of the meeting? What if the individual's discernment is correct? What if the meeting's is correct? What if both are partially correct and partially incorrect? God is not a God of confusion, but of clarity and unity. How should we to seek for God's answer?

William Penn considered this as follows:

Question: *Must I conform to things whether I can receive them or no?*

Answer: No. But now consider the reason thou canst not receive them. Is the fault in the things themselves? Are they inconsistent with Truth or will not the Truth assent unto them? Or is the fault in thee? Is it thy weakness or carelessness? If thy weakness, it is to be borne with, and informed; if thy carelessness, thou oughtest to be admonished. For it is the root of Ranterism to assert that nothing is a duty incumbent upon thee, but what thou art persuaded is thy duty. The seared conscience pleads liberty against all duty, the unenlightened conscience is unconcerned, and the dead conscience is uncondemned unless this distinction be allowed. There may be ignorance from inability or incapacity and ignorance from disobedience and prejudice. So though thou art not to conform to a thing ignorantly, yet thou art seriously to consider why thou art ignorant and what the cause of such ignorance may be. It can't be God; it must be thyself, who hast not yet received a sense for or against the matter about which thou art in doubt.

Question: *Ought I not be left to the grace of God in my own heart?*

Answer: That is of all things most desirable, since they are well left that are there left. Where all are left with the one spirit of Truth, they must be of one mind; they can't be otherwise. So that to plead this against unity is to abuse the very plea. Therefore if thou pleadest against the counsel and spirit of the Lord in other faithful persons under the pretense of being left to this spirit in thyself, thou opposest the spirit to the spirit and pleadest for disunity under the name of liberty.

Question: *But what if I do not presently see that service in a thing that the rest of my brethren agree in? In this case what is my duty, and theirs?*

Answer: It is thy duty to wait upon God in silence and patience, and as thou abide in the simplicity of Truth, thou wilt receive an understanding with the rest of thy brethren about the thing doubted. And it is their duty, whilst thou behavest thyself in meekness, to bear with thee, and carry themselves tenderly and lovingly towards thee.

The enemy is at work to scatter the minds of Friends, by that loose plea, "What hast thou to do with me? Leave me to my freedom and to the grace of God in myself," and the like; but this is a deviation from, and a perversion of, the ancient principle of Truth. For this is the plain consequence of this plea, that anyone, especially if they are but lately convinced, shall say, "I see no evil in declining a public testimony in suffering times or hiding in times of persecution, and no man hath power to reprove me, but I may be as good a Friend as any of you according to my measure." Here is measure set up against measure—which is confusion itself.

The enemy is working to rend and divide the heritage of God who, under the pretense of crying down man, forms, and prescriptions, is crying down the heavenly Man, Christ Jesus and his blessed order and government.

DISCUSSION QUESTIONS:

1. At the beginning of this guide, a framed quote from John H. Curtis explains ways in which Christ leads His people. In that passage, Curtis asserts: "The people of God are the Church of Christ.... Fallible human beings are brought to be a people." What does it mean to be "brought to be a people"? How does the individual's "freedom without anarchy" relate to the group's unity?
2. How do we know if we are out-of-unity because we are right (and the others are wrong) or because we are careless, weak, or otherwise at fault?
3. William Penn warns that we can damage the work of Christ under pretense of refusing outward authority and forms. Why does our obedience to our Lord require us to seek clarity and

unity with our meeting—that group of faithful persons all seeking to live and work in obedience to Christ?
4. What does that obedience require of both us and our meeting? If we cannot find ready unity, what action is incumbent upon us as individuals and a meeting community?
5. In the face of disunity within a meeting, how can we weigh counsel from the various written records of Friends and other Christians, and the words in Scripture?
6. What is resonating most deeply within you?

Section 6.D
Clerking: An Aid for Decision-Making

Reading: Susan S. Smith, "Clerking in the Spirit of Christ," *Sound, Sound Abroad You Faithful Servants! A Call to True Quaker Ministry*, pp. 52-57 (New Foundation Fellowship).

Clerking is a service to God and to the meeting. The clerk's tasks are to organize the meeting's business and to discern and record the truth that is brought forth in the meeting. Although some procedural guidelines can be sketched, rightly ordered clerking involves more than following the rules. Clerking also requires on-the-spot receptivity to God's guidance. In addition, for the clerk to function effectively, the other meeting members must accept and carry out their own responsibilities during the meeting, and all participants must be united in a common faith in God.

Successful clerking starts with an attitude of service. The clerk is selected to help the group recognize the acts and conclusions to which God is calling them. In order to do that well, the clerk needs to prepare for every meeting with private prayer and to come with the intention of serving the meeting in its own service to God.

In some yearly meetings, the two basic services of clerking are separated by appointing both a presiding clerk, who organizes the business, and a recording clerk, who writes the minutes. That separation occurs in the clerking of some of the committees in Ohio Yearly Meeting. However, as yearly meeting clerk, I have felt comfortable to conduct our business sessions in the more traditional manner, having help only with the reading of incoming documents. Nevertheless, for the sake of analysis, let us consider separately the functions of presiding and recording.

Presiding begins with organizing the agenda for a particular session. In our yearly meeting, it is customary to begin with a significant period of waiting worship during which vocal ministry often occurs. I prefer to ask an elder of the meeting to discern when it is time to take up the business, and to make that announcement. The first item thereafter is the reading of a selection from the Bible. The clerk needs to be sensitive to God's guidance in choosing that passage, for the worship and the Scripture reading set a reverent tone for the subsequent business.

The Scripture reading is followed by items of business. It works best to begin the business with a few quick, easy items, and to put important but nondivisive items next. Thus, a basis of successful cooperative working is established. Next, one needs to bring forth any potentially divisive concerns while Friends are still fairly rested and attentive. Finish with matters of less depth, such as housekeeping and scheduling business.

Another aspect of presiding involves facilitating progress through each agenda item to the next one. Each item needs to be introduced, and there may be last-minute changes to the agenda. A second part of this process in some yearly meetings is recognizing speakers. However, in Ohio Yearly Meeting, we do not give the clerk that responsibility, for having the clerk give members permission to speak can interrupt God's motion. We find that it works well to leave that responsibility to all Friends, as it is in a meeting for worship, expecting each Friend to wait to be clear that God's Holy Spirit is indeed prompting the felt urge to speak.

As each Friend is speaking, the clerk must listen to what is being said. That listening must continue whenever anyone is speaking, even if the clerk is also doing something else. Listening to what is being said is the first element of writing a minute.

The second element in writing a good minute is selecting the essence of truth in what is being said. Rarely does one have time to write everything a speaker says, but paraphrasing a summary often sacrifices accuracy. I find that it works best to listen for and write down verbatim one or two sentences at the heart of each message, catching that part of what the speaker says which reflects God's truth. If the words are given to the speaker by God, then retaining those exact words retains God's message. The discernment involved in selecting those words, even as they are being spoken, cannot be accomplished through any outward training or personal effort on my part. When that discernment is at work, it comes as God's gift. When it is not given, I cannot replace it with my own thoughts. The task described thus far is to listen and to select.

The third element in recording a minute is writing down the core of truth from each message; the writing must happen even as one is listening to the rest of the speaker's comments, or to the next speaker. Unless there are noticeable gaps between speakers, the clerk has to be able to write an important point while listening to and selecting from what is being said next. Successful clerking, then, involves not only hearing, choosing, and writing what is important, but also blending those functions into a smooth whole.

The kernels of truth from spoken messages form the basis of the minute reflecting the meeting's decision. However, it is not necessary either to record or to include in the minute a part of every spoken message. Some messages may be redundant; others may be irrelevant. Choosing to omit all of what a particular speaker says should not be done lightly, but that choice is one of the clerk's options in discernment.

The pieces recorded from the various speakers seldom are spoken in the order in which they will fit best in the final document. Writing the minute also involves arranging the several pieces into a logical order, and joining them together with appropriate conjunctions. After several pieces of a minute have been recorded, it is often useful to begin considering the order in which they should be used, while at the same time listening for the next part to write down. A number can be placed in the margin by each statement to indicate its expected order in the finished minute. Statements may have to be reordered as more pieces emerge from spoken messages, but with the ordering process started, it is usually fairly easy to arrive at a completed minute soon after the speaking is finished.

Writing minutes is the task of recording and organizing the elements of truth that the meeting has found. The clerk does this by opening the way for God's gifts through the members and by being watchful for the truth that is given. The clerk is neither the chief executive officer nor the head of the meeting and should resist any suggestion that he or she take that responsibility.

Although the clerk is not the leader of the group, the clerk's actions can have a profound influence on the meeting's ability to be faithful. There are many opportunities for the clerk to err. One common temptation is to try to get the meeting to arrive at a decision the clerk has already selected. It is essential that the clerk come to the session "open," free of any commitment to one side of an issue. It is also important that the clerk refrain from adding his or her understanding on an issue, either by speaking to a matter of business or by inserting in the minute ideas that have not been spoken by someone else. Manipulations such as "standing aside from the table" and then speaking personally are rarely if ever appropriate. One cannot step momentarily aside from clerking and then step back into it.

While the clerk's work influences the meeting's faithfulness, the success of a business meeting depends also on the obedience of the entire body. In some meetings, or on some topics, Friends need to be more willing to verbalize the convictions they feel from the Lord. In other cases, members need to maintain discipline among themselves, speaking only when moved by God, speaking concisely, not quibbling either with each other or with the wording of a minute, and maintaining worshipful silence except when speaking to the business. While it may be helpful to encourage the meeting's elders to be ready to warn against excessive speaking or contention during business, it is important that all Friends feel and exercise corporate responsibility for good order.

Occasionally, it will be necessary for the clerk to act to maintain order. A general comment is best, such as a call for a period of worship, rather than a public admonition to a particular

Friend. It is also sometimes helpful to focus the meeting's attention back to the topic that needs consideration, simply by restating the question at hand.

Sooner or later, it becomes time to reach a conclusion. Obviously, votes are not to be taken, and a simple mental weighing of the support for each perspective on an issue will also usually fail to find the truth. Choosing the lowest common denominator or the few points on which everyone agrees may miss important parts of what should be found. What does it mean to "identify the sense of the meeting"?

The "sense of the meeting" is different from consensus. Consensus is based on everyone's effort to work together to find agreement. The sense of the meeting goes beyond human effort, taking as its basis the conviction that there is in God's plan one right way, which will be opened to those who faithfully seek it. Thus, discovering the sense of the meeting requires that those who would find it be united in a common faith in God and in their intention to be obedient to God's prompting. A sense of the meeting can rarely be found in a secular gathering, nor does it evolve readily in a group with serious theological divisions. However, when meeting members and the clerk are united from the beginning in their essential faith in God, identifying the truth God sets forth is possible. The discerning clerk will be able to pull the right conclusion from the spoken contributions, and the meeting, sensing that rightness, will be able to unite with the minute.

There will, however, be times when the meeting feels that a proposed minute needs to be modified. The clerk may have failed to record an important point, or the wording may need adjusting. When modifications are proposed, the clerk needs to remember his or her position as the servant of God and the meeting. While suggested modifications are occasionally out of right order and should therefore call forth some hesitation, the clerk needs to guard firmly against any feelings of personal ownership of the words that have been written. Modifications should usually be made as requested, without any statements of defense or explanation by the clerk. If the meeting is not in accord with the modification suggested, it is the responsibility of some other member to question the change. Staying apart from any contention allows the clerk to look clearly at the questioning process and to have better opportunity to find the words that will represent unity in the meeting.

Being willing to make modifications to a minute is one way the clerk evidences trust in the process of corporate discernment. The clerk also needs to be fully trusting that the meeting, through its individual members, can listen to God's Voice and speak what is given. Trust should work in the other direction also. As the clerk is successful in sensing and recording the Truth when it is given, the meeting's members come to trust the clerk's gift and self-discipline. Individual Friends then feel little need to plot speaking strategies or to act politically in business meeting, allowing much more room for God to be heard and heeded.

Throughout the whole process, it is important that everyone be comfortable with periods of silence. The clerk should not worry if no one says anything for a while. Everyone may be seeking God's guidance. Similarly, Friends need to be willing to wait in prayerful silence while the clerk completes a minute. Those prayers may be a necessary part of the clerk's finding the right words. Silent waiting worship provides an effective vehicle for God's work among Friends, in business meeting as well as in meeting for worship.

In summary, clerking ability is a gift from God. Able clerking involves simultaneous listening, selecting, and writing, and it cannot be done in one's own strength. Meeting members must exercise discipline over their own participation, speaking when prompted by God and not speaking otherwise. Coming in gospel order to the sense of the meeting requires that meeting members share with the clerk an active, obedient faith in the power of Almighty God to guide them into corporate understanding of the Truth they need to know.

DISCUSSION QUESTIONS:

1. Why is seeking God's will the ground and foundation of Friends' business procedure?
2. Have you witnessed an instance of God's ability to bring a divided meeting into unity? Please explain.
3. What aspects of a good business meeting are compromised if the clerk stands aside from the table and offers his or her own ideas on an item of business?
4. What are the advantages and disadvantages of having the meeting itself be the primary human keeper of order during business meeting, rather than the clerk? What can be done to encourage a sense of *corporate* responsibility for keeping the business under God's direction?
5. In what ways is the clerk not the CEO of the meeting? Are there any CEO functions that a clerk should perform?
6. Can you identify spiritual gifts that a meeting might look for as it seeks a clerk?
7. What can a meeting do to foster the development of clerking gifts that some members may have?

Section 6.E
The Advices and Queries

Reading: Carole Edgerton Treadway. "The Queries of North Carolina Yearly Meeting (Conservative) 1809 – 1983" in the *Journal of the North Carolina Yearly Meeting (Conservative)*, #2, Winter 2003.

The Advices

Examining ourselves as individuals and as a community. Carole Edgerton Treadway, in the *Journal of North Carolina Yearly Meeting (Conservative)*, explains some of the history of the use of queries among Friends:

> The custom of allowing ourselves to be queried and to answer as honestly as we can is one of the most distinctive features of Quaker practice. It originated in the early days of Quakerism, although the Queries became institutionalized only in the eighteenth century when formal Disciplines were adopted.... Very early, George Fox introduced some guidelines for the orderly functioning of the new meetings that were emerging out of the creative chaos of the earliest years. In 1656, there was a gathering of elders at Balby in Yorkshire at which these guidelines were adopted.... These guidelines came to be known as "Advices."

Friends Advices today represent the wisdom and experience of Friends collected over time. Advices are directive but, as their name implies, they are not a set of rules as in many churches, nor do they prescribe belief as a creed would. The Advices are a container, holding the shape of the Religious Society of Friends. They reveal the characteristics of life in a community that seeks to function under divine guidance. The Advices indicate the broad outlines of shared faith and practice that give meaning and purpose to the lives of those who commit themselves to their discipline. Following the Advices helps to establish a community in "gospel order" and, over the course of a lifetime, brings each follower closer into unity with God and with neighbor—however defined.

Advices reflect the values and convictions of the yearly meeting that publishes them. They provide a vehicle for individual members' self-evaluation in regard to "all various principles and testimonies which should guide our daily lives." (*The Book of Discipline of Ohio Yearly Meeting*, 2008. p. 20) The following are some of the advices used in Ohio Yearly Meeting (for a complete list, see *The Book of Discipline of Ohio Yearly Meeting*, available at www.OhioYearlyMeeting.org):

> Use vigilant care, dear Friends, not to overlook those promptings of love and truth which you may feel in your hearts, for these are the tender leadings of the Spirit of God. Nor should any of us resist God's workings within us, for it is His redemptive love which strives to show us our darkness, and to lead us to true repentance and to His marvelous light. "Behold, I stand at the door and knock: if any man hear my voice and open the door, I will come in to him, and will sup with him, and he with me" (Rev.3:20).

> Be faithful in maintaining your testimony against all war as inconsistent with the Spirit and teaching of Christ. Live in the Life and Power that takes away the occasions of all wars and strife. Seek to take your part in the ministry of reconciliation between individuals, groups, and nations. Let the law of kindness know no limits. Show a loving consideration for all people.

> Carefully maintain truthfulness and sincerity in your conduct, and encourage the same in your families. In your

style of living, in your dress, and in the furniture of your houses, choose what is simple, useful, and good.

Be diligent in the reading of the Bible and other spiritually helpful writings. Gather daily in your families for worship. Such times have a special value in bringing little children especially into the experience of united worship, and so preparing them for the larger meeting for worship, as they learn in the silence to bow to the power of God.

Follow steadfastly after all that is pure and lovely and of good report. Be prayerful. Be watchful. Be humble. Let no failure discourage you. When temptation comes, make it an opportunity to gain new strength by standing fast, that you may enter into that life of gladness and victory to which all are called.

Seek for your children that full development of God's gifts which true education can bring about. Remember that the service to which we are called needs healthy bodies, trained minds, high ideals, and an understanding of the laws and purposes of God. Give of your best to the study of the Bible, and the understanding of the Christian faith. Be open-minded, ready constantly to receive new light.

When we gather together in worship, let us remember that there is committed to us, as disciples of Christ, a share in the priesthood. We should help one another, whether in silence, or through spoken word, or prayer. Let none of us assume that vocal ministry is never to be our part. If the call comes, there should be no quenching of the Spirit. The sense of our own unworthiness must not exempt us from this service, nor must the fear of being unable to find the right words, "for it shall be given you in that same hour what ye shall speak" (Matt.10:19).

The Queries

Carole Treadway explains how the Queries developed:

> The Queries were drawn from the Advices and were answered informally until the middle of the eighteenth century. At that time, there was growing concern that Friends were sliding into a secular manner of living and becoming nominal Friends only. Those who bore this concern inspired a widespread reemphasis on observing the Advices, and Friends began answering the Queries formally.

The following queries are some of those used in Ohio Yearly Meeting (for a complete list, see *The Book of Discipline of Ohio Yearly Meeting* at www.OhioYearlyMeeting.org):

> Are meetings for worship well and punctually attended? Is our behavior therein conducive to meditation and communion with God? Do we maintain a waiting spiritual worship and a free gospel ministry? Do we welcome others to share this fellowship with us?

> Do we cherish a forgiving spirit, and strive to "walk in love as Christ also hath loved us"? Is each one of us careful for the reputation of others? Are we mindful to love our neighbor as ourselves? If differences threaten to disrupt the Christian harmony between the members, is prompt action taken?

> Do we observe simplicity in our manner of living, sincerity in speech, and modesty in apparel? Do we guard against involving ourselves in temporal affairs to the hindrance of spiritual growth? Are we just in our dealings and careful to fulfill our promises? Do we seek to make our Christian faith part of our daily work?

Believing our bodies to be the temple of God (see 1 Corinthians 3:16). Are we concerned to attain a high level of physical and mental health? To this end, are our lives examples of temperance in all things? Do we avoid and discourage the use and handling of intoxicants, tobacco, and improper use of drugs?

Are our homes places of peace, joy, and contentment? Are they an influence for good in the neighborhood, community, and country? Do we set a good Christian example for our children to follow? Are Friends careful that their children realize that our loving Savior will faithfully guide them through life, as they are willing to accept and obey Him? Do we help our children to read and appreciate the Bible?

DISCUSSION QUESTIONS:

1. What would be the effects of restating the Advices as rules?
2. What does it mean to have a "shared faith and practice"?
3. Are there any of the above Advices that you find especially relevant or interesting? Explain.
4. On a personal level, how would/do you feel when giving your own query answer to the entire meeting? What accountability is implied?
5. On a more general level, what do you think about OYM's process of query answering? How can that process support spiritual and meeting community growth? What problems might/do arise, and how could they be removed or reduced?
6. What is resonating most deeply within you?

Section 6.F
Spirit-Led Teachers

Readings: 2 Timothy 3:16-17; Robert Barclay, *Apology for the True Christian Divinity,*Prop. 3, § V-VI (Freiday).

After explaining that being led by Christ's Spirit is the essence of Christianity, Barclay describes the role of Spirit-led human teachers:

> Although God leads us chiefly by his Spirit, sometimes he conveys his comfort and consolation by a word written or spoken [by another person] at an opportune time. By it, the faithful are made instruments in the hand of the Lord to strengthen and encourage one another. This also tends to foster their growth and lead them to salvation. Those who are led by the Spirit naturally love and cherish the things which represent the product of the Spirit in other persons. They also find that such mutual manifestations of the heavenly life also tend to quicken the mind and to provide the recollection of truth so necessary for the progress of the gospel....
>
> God teaches his people himself; and nothing is made clearer than the fact that under the New Covenant, no human teacher is needed[6]. In spite of this, one of the major results of Christ's ascension was the sending of teachers and pastors for perfecting the faithful. The same work is ascribed to them as to the Scriptures. Both are primarily for the development of greater maturity in the faith of those who believe. But human

---

[6] See Jeremiah 31:31f.

teachers are by no means to have preference over the teaching of God Himself under the New Covenant.

DISCUSSION QUESTIONS:

1. Even though no human teachers are "necessary" under the New Covenant, we find it helpful to have God speak to us through other humans. Barclay says this encourages us in a way that, apparently, being taught only inwardly does not. What has been your experience with the Holy Spirit teaching you through others?
2. What is resonating most deeply within you?

Section 6.G
Eldering and Oversight

Readings: 1 Corinthians 12; Seth Hinshaw. "A Plea for Strong Eldership" 3/28/2010 in *Chronicler's Minutiae* at http://chronicler-3.blogspot.com; "Summary and Some Implications for Eldering" Charles Thomas, in *Friends Consultation on Eldering*, Richmond, Indiana. December 9-12, 1982 (see also previous 2 pages); *So that You Come Behind in No Gift: Ohio Yearly Meeting's Gathering on Eldering 6/20-22/1996.* Ohio Yearly Meeting; *A Description of the Qualifications Necessary to a Gospel Minister.* Samuel Bownas. Pendle Hill Publications, 1989.

Friends recognize that eldering and oversight, like ministry and teaching, are gifts provided by God for the accomplishment of God's work within and beyond meetings and churches. Let us consider eldering and oversight each in turn.

Eldering involves encouraging another person or a whole group to faithfulness—that is, to putting faith into practice. Eldering is encouraging others to hear, trust, and follow God. Having our daily life reflect our faith requires discernment of God's ongoing guidance and then obedience to it. A person may feel, "I want to be faithful, but how do I know what God wants? And how do I manage to do what I know I should?" Eldering helps answer those questions.

Eldering happens at the interface of inward faith and outward action. Eldering helps with *discernment*—knowing right from wrong; with *motivation*—doing what you know is right; with *caution*—waiting for clearness before acting. Eldering offers *feedback*—a gentle reprimand for something wrong or an affirmation of something done right; provides *recognition and development of others' gifts;* and *supports a spiritual climate* in which ministry and personal spiritual growth can flourish.

Some people are uneasy with the idea that Friends can help each other distinguish between acts that are spiritually right and those that are wrong. However, in various work situations, colleagues help each other figure out and then follow through with doing what is right on particular tasks. In community groups, friends help each other identify and then use right approaches to child-raising, food preparation, and much more. Eldering involves similar help with choices that have spiritual ramifications.

Eldering is often specific and personal. Ministry given in meeting for worship might offer a general caution about being tempted into greed or pride. Eldering would more typically involve saying to someone privately, "I think your new job sounds wonderful, but with that big salary, are you going to be able to maintain your simple lifestyle?" Or, to a minister who has given a good message during worship, an elder might say, "What you said today had the ring of Truth. I am thankful for God's work within you." The recipient of good eldering feels the rightness of it. Even when eldering contains an element of correction, it contains the sense of truth.

The person who elders. An act of true eldering is a gift from God to be used for the spiritual encouragement of the person or the group receiving such counsel. A person who is often given that gift is called an elder, just as a person who has a reliable gift of teaching is called a teacher, and one who ministers frequently during worship is a minister.

Elders are discerners of character and motives. They can separate right from wrong, truth from untruth. Elders need to be tactful, to be cheerful and not severe, to be trustworthy, to be calm in the midst of a spiritual tempest. Elders grow to have a large reserve of wisdom from which to draw. Elders need to be constantly watchful over themselves, that their own agendas not interfere with their calling, yet they must be diligent for right gospel order. They need to be supportive of those who are spiritually struggling. A person living into his or her gift of eldering provides a good example—of humility, right choices, and repentance. Elders must be willing to talk about what is happening spiritually within themselves.

Some Friends struggle against the idea that over a period of time, certain people are used more frequently by God for vocal ministry, some are used more often for eldering, and some are used only occasionally for either ministry or eldering but are used by God for other types of service. We may want to turn our understanding that "anyone can be used in vocal ministry or eldering" into an assertion that "everyone will be equally used." However, we do not have much trouble recognizing, encouraging, and appreciating individual gifts in music, sports, healing, etc. We easily say, "She is a gifted musician" or "He is a true athlete." The meeting and its individual members should also be alert to signs of consistently operating spiritual gifts.

Nurturing new gifts. Publicly identifying individuals with particular spiritual gifts can help those individuals grow in their gifts. It can also help people in the meeting know whom to ask for particular spiritual help. Friends with the gift of eldering are often especially sensitive to signs of a spiritual gift arising in others. Established elders can be helpful in nurturing new gifts. Although any person can be used in ministry, eldering, or oversight, people with one of those particular gifts carry out that service more effectively and can benefit more from sensitive mentoring. Furthermore, a person's spiritual gift is likely to develop more fully in a setting where other people have and practice that gift.

It is often easier for a meeting to identify a person's gift of ministry than to recognize a gift of eldering. One reason for that difference lies in the natures of ministry and eldering. Ministry is usually accomplished publicly, taking place for everyone to notice in a meeting for worship. Eldering, on the other hand, is more often done privately between the elder and one or two other people. Therefore, meetings and the established elders in them should be especially alert for developing elders. Asking "Who is good at helping others with spiritual problems?" will often identify an elder.

Eldering and the meeting. The gift of eldering, like all spiritual gifts, works in the context of the body of Christ. That context includes a shared conviction that Jesus speaks in our hearts in a unifying way, calling us to follow Him. An elder is not free to make up or privately discern between right and wrong, or to launch out in a personal effort to "fix" some problem. Eldering based on the elder's own ideas is wrong and will not bear good fruit. Each elder needs to understand and work from the meeting's corporate faith and discernment. Unity of basic faith within the meeting not only is a foundation for each elder's actions but also opens the way for recipients to appreciate the eldering that comes their way.

It is best for elders to live among the community of believers, attending its meetings and remaining aware of what is happening among the people on an everyday basis. Elders need contact with others called to that office, both in their own monthly meeting and in the quarterly and yearly meeting. Younger elders learn from older elders just by being together.

In formally recognizing a member's spiritual gift, a Friends' meeting is saying that the person's gift has come to its attention and the meeting affirms its presence. Formal acknowledgement of a gift helps gifted persons understand what is going on with them spiritually, and it makes it easier for Friends mature in a particular gift to nurture beginners. In that way, the meeting encourages the person to let God develop the gift for use in God's work in the meeting and beyond.

Sometimes the entire meeting itself needs eldering. The meeting needs guidance, just as individuals do, to remember its principles and keep listening to God. Elders are sometimes called to encourage the whole meeting to faithfulness. Elders do that by praying for the meeting during worship or business; providing for right order during meetings; signaling the close of meetings for worship; keeping principles clear during times of decision-making; organizing times for meeting prayer, healing, discussion, work, etc., as needed; discerning and calling out gifts for the benefit of the whole meeting;

and keeping open their own "inward listening space toward God" for the meeting's condition.

Elders also have a special concern for and relationship with ministers. They encourage ministers in their vocal ministry, often in private discussion and also through correspondence. Elders are often useful as companions for Friends traveling for ministry or planned speaking engagements. Not having functioning elders in a meeting takes a toll on the ministry and spiritual life of the meeting. In fact, it has been said that if Friends want more inspired ministry in their meetings for worship, they should seek first to identify and encourage the elders among them.

Dangers and support for elders. It is essential that eldering be done under God's guidance. Doing what is technically right without God's direction leads to trouble, as does confusing one's own desires with those of God. The elder must also guard against developing assumptions that certain people are always right—or always wrong. A similar challenge involves maintaining an appropriate balance between supporting the functioning of the meeting as a whole and addressing the needs of individuals. In the past, elders enforced community standards; often today, individual perceptions are emphasized over group needs. Both extremes are harmful to spiritual wholeness. Elders need to be able to maintain confidences, but they must also discern accurately when to seek another elder's help with a complex problem.

As we have seen, elders should not undertake their work "in their own strength." Elders themselves need the support of good eldering, both in their personal lives and in their service as elders. In addition to spiritually encouraging ministers, other individuals, and the meeting as a body, elders work with each other. In Ohio Yearly Meeting, that work is facilitated by regular meetings of ministers, elders, and overseers together, where challenges can be shared confidentially and advice given.

Oversight and overseers. The third spiritual gift that Ohio Yearly Meeting recognizes is that of oversight. The gift of oversight involves awareness of and care for the physical context in which God's work takes place. This includes following through on the meeting's interest in the basic physical well-being of its members, assuring that all members have sufficient food, a place to live, and medical care. The duties of "hospitality" and "buildings" committees can also be seen as oversight. As the minutes of one of OYM's monthly meetings noted in 2001,

> The overseer has a special gift to meet needs of an outward nature among the Lord's flock. The overseer, when functioning properly, can be seen as the hands of the Lord at work. The overseer exhibits concern for living life in this world. The overseers should show good judgment and wisdom, tact and kindliness, and sensitivity in love to the temporal needs of others.
>
> Members may find it helpful to consult with an overseer on important decisions they face, such as may be involved in changing jobs, educational questions, counseling needs, marital problems or other questions of family living, matters of health, or the making of major purchases. Overseers should not make others feel inadequate but should give help in the spirit of sharing in the Lord. Sometimes a few short minutes of oversight may make a difference; at other times lengthy sessions are needed.
>
> Overseers should always work discreetly and often may need to work privately with individuals. A fund should be available for overseers to use at their discretion to help with outward needs as may be required. Overseers themselves need to exhibit good stewardship and management of resources, as an example to others.

Ministry, eldering, and oversight compared. The Ohio Yearly Meeting minute quoted just above continues:

> There are not sharp distinctions to be made among the three offices (minister, elder, overseer), but their differences are those of emphasis.... Ministers are called to express, especially vocally, the message of God; elders encourage the indwelling of the Lord's Spirit; and overseers help put the Lord's message to work in our outward lives. A blending of the three is necessary for the good functioning of the meeting in our Lord's business.

The three offices draw on different gifts or types of authority: the gift of ministry involves prophetic authority (speaking in response to God's Voice within in order to make known God's will to others, not foretelling future events); eldering is based on the authority of discernment; and oversight involves pastoral care.

While the gift of ministry involves giving vocal messages during worship, Friends with a gift of eldering may also give messages fairly often. The difference between typical messages from a minister and those from an elder is one of style rather than frequency. Ministers' messages are usually broad and extensive, developing several points fully. Elders are typically succinct, offering a few sentences that get quickly to the heart of the message. Overseers, like all other members of the meeting, will probably give anointed messages in worship from time to time, but they usually live into their particular gift by doing rather than by speaking.

Ministry is typically focused on increasing the hearers' *faith*—that is, on encouraging right beliefs and an immediate relationship with God. Eldering focuses on increasing *faithfulness*—that is, acting in harmony with one's beliefs. Oversight arranges circumstances and gives advice with the aim of supporting spiritual growth. Those different points of focus can be represented as God's Truth (ministry), God's Way (eldering) and God's Life (oversight) (see

John 14:6). They do, however, overlap and blend together. For instance, a career decision often involves both practical, economic questions and concerns about how the job will mesh with the person's religious convictions. A person with the gift of oversight will probably emphasize one set of questions while an elder will look at the situation from a different perspective.

Ministry often emphasizes content, eldering emphasizes process, and oversight emphasizes practicality. Ministry is public and general; eldering is typically private and personal. Oversight is more likely to be practiced personally and perhaps privately, such as when an overseer's help is sought for financial or job-related questions. Some overseers' work is more public, such as arranging hospitality for visitors or a workday for a meeting family overcome by illness.

The differences among the three gifts can also be illustrated with various images. For instance, the minister may be seen as a mother giving birth and delivering God's message. The midwife (elder) stays nearby, encouraging, admonishing, and explaining what is happening. The overseer has been on hand ahead of time, getting the room and supplies ready and remains present to make sure those things are in order. An example from animal husbandry provides different images. The minister pours appropriate feed (according to God's guidance) into a trough where the animals can readily consume it. The elder offers guidance toward nourishment and safety, herding the animals to the right pasture and away from danger. The overseer has again been busy beforehand, tilling and fertilizing fields and maintaining needed fences in good repair.

The information in this comparison of the three gifts is summarized in the table on the following two pages:

TYPICAL DIFFERENCES BETWEEN MINISTRY, ELDERING, AND OVERSIGHT

Compiled by Susan Smith, 4-2001

	MINISTRY	ELDERING	OVERSIGHT
Type of gift	Prophetic	Discerning	Pastoral
Vocal messages in worship	Broad, extensive	Succinct	
Focus	Increasing faith: Encouraging right beliefs and immediate relationship with God	Increasing faithfulness: encouraging acting in and from right beliefs	Creating supportive physical environment or context
Message conveyed	God's Truth	God's Way	God's Life
Emphasis (usually, not always)	Content	Process	Practicality
Mode (usually)	Public, general	Private, personal	Both

	MINISTRY	ELDERING	OVERSIGHT
Part of the "body" emphasized	Mouth (speaking)	Ear (listening)	Hand (making)
Birthing image	Mother – Delivering God's message	Midwife – Encouraging, admonishing, clarifying; maintaining right conditions for "birth"	Assistant – Preparing bed, supplies and equipment
Agricultural image	Pouring feed into trough	Guiding into green pastures and away from thorns	Fertilizing & tilling fields; repairing fences

DISCUSSION QUESTIONS

1. How do you respond to the suggestions in this section that elders are spiritual nurturers?
2. How would having elders be helpful in your meeting? How might it be problematic?
3. Do you recognize gifts in Friends in your meeting when you consider the chart above?
4. What is most resonating with you here?

Chapter 7
FAITHFUL LIVING

Section 7.A
Our Lives as Our Testimony

Readings: Matthew 5-7; 1 Corinthians 13; Ephesians 4:17-31; Colossians 3; The Book of James; 1 John 3:11-24.

Testimony versus testimonies. Testimony means "evidence in support of a fact, proof." It also can mean "a public declaration regarding a religious experience." Most people who have attended evangelical services have heard the latter, when individuals rise and tell their personal stories of coming to faith in Jesus Christ. Friends through the first three centuries of their existence embraced both definitions, recognizing that Christ Jesus and the Scriptures enjoin us to witness not only with our tongues, but also with our lives. "Not everyone who says to me, 'Lord, Lord,' will enter the kingdom of heaven, but only he who does the will of my Father who is in heaven. Many will say to me on that day, 'Lord, Lord, did we not prophesy in your name, and in your name drive out demons and perform many miracles?' Then I will tell them plainly, 'I never knew you. Away from me, you evildoers!'" (Matthew 7:21-23).

True faith produces good fruit. The apostle James declares, "What good is it, my brothers and sisters, if someone claims to have faith but has no deeds? Can such faith save them? Suppose a brother or a sister is without clothes and daily food. If one of you says to them, 'Go in peace; keep warm and well fed,' but does nothing about their physical needs, what good is it? In the same way, faith by itself, if it is not accompanied by action, is dead" (James 2:14-17). The apostle Paul is clear concerning the fruits of the Spirit: "love, joy, peace, forbearance, kindness, goodness, faithfulness, gentleness and self-control" (Galatians 5:22-23). Faith that produces no visible works lacks the concreteness of truth, and Paul warns (1 Corinthians

13) that, though we be eloquent as the angels and give up our bodies to martyrdom, if we have not love, we do these things for nothing.

Among twentieth-century Friends, it became popular to speak of testimonies, rather than testimony. Many writers and scholars developed lists of testimonies that they termed "Friends' testimonies," such as sincerity, honesty, integrity, peaceableness, faithfulness, etc. While such analyses help remind us of the fruits expected of us, they also had the unintended consequences of laying out a "smorgasbord" that led some Friends to pick and choose a few testimonies that they would uphold, and that led some others to emphasize certain "testimonies" as far more important than others.

Let us return from the fragmented vision of "testimonies" to the original Friends' understanding that our entire lives are to be a testimony—a proof—of the presence and power of Christ Jesus alive in the world. This is what Christ Jesus and his apostles repeatedly exhort us to in the Scriptures: Ephesians 4:17-31; Colossians 3; 1 John 3:11-24, and a multitude of other passages.

DISCUSSION QUESTIONS:

1. What personal experiences can you cite that reflect the danger of emphasizing some testimonies as more important than others?
2. We have all witnessed much hypocrisy on the part of those who do not practice what they preach, and the temptation is to go to the opposite extreme, of emphasizing practice to the disregard of speaking of our faith. What are the dangers of relying solely on one's example to carry one's Christian message and neglecting to speak of our faith?
3. Why is seeing our Christian witness as a seamless garment, rather than a patchwork of individual virtues, important?
4. What is resonating most deeply in you now?

Section 7.B
The Lamb's War

Readings: *Jack Smith. The Lamb's War: A Presentation to the General Gathering of Conservative Friends, 6/17/2006,* Barnesville, OH, *www.michiganquakers.org/lamb.oym.htm;Selections from the Writings of James Nayler*, third edition, Brian Drayton, editor.

The Lamb's War defined. Early Friends identified the struggle between Christ Jesus and the Satanic powers of darkness and evil as the Lamb's War. It is a war to expose and judge the Deceiver and his deceptions *both within each of us individually and in the world at large.* The first generations of Friends understood, far better than the generations that followed them, that Christ's inward work of sanctifying each of us was as essential in the conversion of the world as was bringing others into God's kingdom. Too often since the seventeenth century, the emphasis has shifted back and forth between the inward struggle and the outward conflict with evil, with the result that Christ's work has suffered from a want of a clear, sustained, and zealous witness.

In the Old Testament, the lamb is a symbol of the people of God (Exodus 12:1-13) and a figure foretelling the sacrifice of Jesus (Gen 22:12-18; Isaiah 53:7). The lamb as a figure for Jesus Christ continues in the New Testament (John 1:36; Acts 8:32-33; 1 Peter 1:18-19). Revelation refers to the Lamb as Christ in a number of verses and to the struggle of the forces of Satan with the Lamb (6:15-17; 12:10-11).

In referring to "the Lamb's War," early Friends were not referring to an abstract theological concept but a reality they experienced in all areas of their lives, as through conviction they abstained from oaths, military service, the payment of tithes, superfluous fashions, and dishonest dealings. The Lamb's War allowed no room for lukewarm commitment. Early Friends understood that Jesus Christ was leading them, providing them spiritual weapons and sustaining them as they submitted to "the cross of Christ, which is the power of God ..." (G. Fox, Epistle 222, 1662).

The primary battleground. The Lamb's War is, first and foremost, an inward war in which the inward enemy is the man or woman of sin within us, our own disobedience in not following God's commandments. To neglect the war within us is to undermine and betray the war effort beyond us. The Enemy of our souls and of our peace, even after our conversion, holds at least some territory within us. Though he was driven from his headship within us when we ceded ourselves to Christ Jesus, the remnants of the old man or woman of disobedience are still deeply entrenched in some areas of our nature, well camouflaged, and extremely subtle and devious, almost as subtle and devious at times as the Evil One who originally seduced and occupied us and whose designs and desires most of us have served far too long.

The Kingdom for which we struggle. The country we fight for is no earthly country, but our Lord's own kingdom. Jesus Himself testified before Pilate: "My kingdom is not of this world. If it were, my servants would fight to prevent my arrest..., but now my kingdom is from another place" (John 18:36). Christ's kingdom is first and foremost a kingdom of truth and "everyone on the side of truth" listens to Him (John 18:37). Jesus is emphatic on this: Only those who do "the will of my Father" will enter the kingdom and be members of it (Matthew 7:21). Even if one prophesies powerfully (or as Paul says, "speaks with the tongues of men and of angels"), casts out demons, and works miracles, if these things are done outside God's will, they mean nothing. They are simply the work of evil doers whom our Lord does not know. Martyrs who have not God's love in them are nothing.

Who is our enemy? Paul was clear and precise in identifying the Enemy. "Our struggle is not against flesh and blood," not against our fellow men and women, "but against the rulers, against the authorities, against the powers of this dark world and against the spiritual forces of evil in the heavenly realms" (Ephesians 6:12).

The weapons we use. Our Lord has clearly defined the weapons we are to bring to His confrontation of evil. As we aren't at war with men and women, our weapons are neither carnal (physical) nor hurtful to any of the creation. As we are at war with "the spiritual forces of evil," we are commanded to use only spiritual weapons. Paul exhorts us to "put on the full armor of God so that you can take your stand against the devil's schemes" (Eph. 6: 10-18). The primary purpose of armor has been to protect the wearer against the weapons and assaults of the enemy. Given the power and viciousness of our enemy, we need to be well protected, "so that when the day of evil comes," we may be able to stand our ground and after we have done everything, "stand firm ... with the belt of truth buckled" around our waist, "with the breastplate of righteousness in place," and with our "feet fitted with the readiness that comes from the gospel of peace." We are to take up the shield of faith with which we can extinguish all the flaming arrows of the evil one and the helmet of salvation and the sword of the Spirit. This is considerable armor and excellent protection, unless we have ignored and neglected our Armorer's directions, His preparations in suiting us, and His careful training and formation. Our very life will be easily taken without faith to protect our head, righteousness to protect our heart and faith to protect us against vital inward life, feet properly shod for the long and difficult marches we face. Our weapons, the gospel of peace and the sword of the Spirit, cut to the Enemy's quick and even if we physically die in the confrontation, we will continue to live as our Lord lives.

DISCUSSION QUESTIONS:

1. Friends today often see the Lamb's War as only an outward struggle against injustice and evil. What dangers do we risk when we separate the world's outward problems from our own struggle with the sin within us? Can we confuse our own partisan political and national agendas with the Lamb's War? How might we avoid this danger?
2. The goal of the Lamb's War is the conversion of the entire world to our Lord Jesus Christ and His will. When Friends ignore this goal, what do they lose? Can the Lamb's War within be pursued in isolation from the Lamb's War without?
3. How have you experienced the Lamb's War within you? What spiritual struggles have you faced?
4. Do we feel called to be instruments for the conversion of anyone?

Section 7.C
The Lamb's War and Peace

Readings: *Special Note: It is imperative that the following Scripture passages be read before Chapter 7.C is studied and kept at hand as the chapter is discussed.* Jeremiah 31:31-34; Isaiah 2:2-4; Isaiah 11:1-9; Ephesians 6:10-17.

As Friends, we believe we are called to follow the leading of God, both as individuals and as a people. It is not for us to set our agendas and then expect God to arrange things so that all comes out in a desirable way. But how are we to know what God's intentions are for us individually and as a people? We look to Jesus, both in the record in Scripture and as He speaks to us today.

By His coming, Jesus ushered in a new era with a New Covenant between God and His people. Prior to Jesus' birth on earth, many prophecies had been given about the nature of this new relationship and how God's people were to live. A most basic one is in Jeremiah 31: 31-34. In Isaiah we find many more prophecies about the coming of Christ and the nature of His revelation to his people. Among those prophecies, Isaiah 2: 2-4 and Isaiah 11:1-9, which describe the peaceable nature of Christ's Kingdom, have been important to Friends over the years. Jesus fulfilled these prophecies. In His teachings and in His behavior Jesus illustrated that outward carnal weapons are not to be used to achieve the goals of His kingdom.

Nevertheless, Friends have used the image of war to demonstrate that obedience to God involves a struggle of epic proportions between good and evil, played out by individuals and corporately by His people. The metaphor of the Lamb's War provides a seemingly contradictory picture of a vulnerable, defenseless animal successfully engaging in combat on a vast scale. The method of the Lamb's War may seem contradictory as well. How can a war achieve the peaceable Kingdom of God and His rule over His creation? To achieve this Kingdom requires a struggle between the followers of Jesus Christ and the forces of this world which oppose Him and His righteousness.

In the Lamb's War, persons allied with Christ acknowledge Him as their leader who sets the goals, properly equips His army of followers, and provides the way to victory. Not only do we have to set aside our own agendas, but we also have to relinquish our attachments to the forces and ways of this world and become as pilgrims in our passage through this life. We have to abandon our personal strengths and abilities in order to accept powerlessness and vulnerability, that the power and strength of Jesus Christ might effectively equip us (Ephesians 6: 10-17). We learn to feel a confidence that is not our own. As the Lamb leads us, He achieves the victory.

The basis of our peace testimony, then, is not that of a secular, humanist belief in the inherent goodness of humans, nor is it a political objective. Neither do we believe in the idea of a just war, which was set forth by Augustine in the fifth century as the basis for Christians to go to outward battle with outward weapons to fight with the armies of this world. Rather, as followers of Jesus Christ, we feel called to obedience to our Master who commanded His disciple to put up his sword. We feel called to seek for the good of all and to achieve a better way that will endure. As George Fox observed, "That which is won by the sword must be upheld by the sword and that which is won by the Spirit will be upheld by the Spirit."

DISCUSSION QUESTIONS:

1. How, if at all, should Friends today be engaged in a struggle against the ways of the world that seem contrary to Christ's ways?
2. What forces and ways of this world do you cling to?
3. Do you see ways that Christ uses to achieve His goals that are different from the ways you might choose?

4. What does it mean to be a "pilgrim" in our passage through this life?
5. When is it easy and when is it harder for you to let yourself be vulnerable? What do we do to keep ourselves from being vulnerable?

Section 7.D
The Peace Testimony: Common Misunderstandings

Reading: Terry H.S. Wallace, "Stand and Live in That Which Takes Away the Occasion for Wars: A Critical Examination of the Quaker Peace Testimony: Present and Past"; Martin Luther King, "Pilgrimage to Nonviolence," *Stride Toward Freedom: The Montgomery Story – Birth of Successful Non-Violent Resistance*, p. 77-95.

A half century ago, Martin Luther King, Jr., observed the tendency of many of those who espouse peace toward shallow self-righteousness, facile thinking, and subtle belligerence toward those who were thoughtful, sensitive conscientious combatants:

> Many pacifists, I felt, failed to see [humanity's] potential for evil, the complexity of man's social involvement, and the glaring reality of collective evil. All too many had an unwarranted optimism concerning man and leaned unconsciously toward self- righteousness.... I came to see the pacifist position not as sinless but as the lesser evil in the circumstances. I felt then, and I feel now, that the pacifist would have a greater appeal if he did not claim to be free from the moral dilemmas that the Christian non-pacifist confronts (King, *Stride Toward Freedom: The Montgomery Story - Birth of Successful Non-Violent Resistance*, p. 81).

While we may take issue with some aspects of King's analysis, his charges concerning "unwarranted optimism" and "self-righteousness" are well worth examining today. The attacks on America on 9/11/2001 have been termed a "wake-up" call for America, and also might well be seen as the same for the Religious Society of Friends, a wake-up call in the case of Friends to reexamine the foundation of its peace witness. Though the U.S. government had warned us over ten years earlier that we were entering an even more dangerous world than the one we had just finished facing during the Cold War, in the absence of worldwide superpower conflict we found that very difficult to believe. We ignored enemies who declared openly that they intended to bring us massive suffering and death. We dreamed such an event was no longer possible.

Even after 9/11, some Friends had great difficulty grasping the reality of an enemy with no interest in negotiation and compromise, an enemy whose inveterate hatred was dedicated to terror and destruction. And some had even greater difficulty grasping that the 9/11 attack had initiated a new war. One such Friend after 9/11 expressed his total puzzlement over why the media and people in general were talking about a "new war." Apparently, he believed a nation's government could ignore the destruction of 3000 citizens' lives and 100 billion-plus dollars in national wealth—and still survive. Quaker officialdom soon developed a rather problematic slogan for the first decade of the new millennium—"War is not the answer." It only raises the question, "Then what is the answer?!" and murmuring, "peace" is not enough. How do we get there?

Other Friends and non-Friends—more partisan and ideological—claimed the essential problem was America itself. This led them to denounce the government, to blame the victims, to make the unhappy self-righteous accusation of "You had it coming to you." They marginalized themselves in their fellow citizens' minds as insensitive, hateful, even disloyal.

However, most Friends reacted like so many other thoughtful and fair-minded Americans: with fear and anger, pain and confusion. One Friend spoke in meeting for worship of his horror as he stood on a roof across from New York City on 9/11 and witnessed the atrocity. The ensuing days added to the trauma as his professional associates, well educated and generally gentle, declared their passionate desire to see the enemy "nuked." This Friend confessed confusion and helplessness, and he was certainly not alone. A

Religious Society whose membership over the last twenty years often declared that its one consistent characteristic was devotion to the Peace Testimony found itself suddenly far less certain of, and unified in, its witness.

An Ungrounded Testimony

For many Friends today, the Peace Testimony has largely become a secular, partisan movement that supports very worldly agendas, and that is based on the belief that we can control our own destiny. Four major erroneous points often made concerning that witness are:

1. *"The Peace Testimony is the one key testimony all Friends can and should agree upon."*

A quick survey of Friends—past and present—will immediately reveal that many Friends did not, and still do not, embrace this witness. Even many Yearly Meeting Faith and Practice books reflect this by blessing both the conscientious combatant and conscientious objector positions.

However, the essential reason the "one key testimony" claim is fallacious lies in the fact that the peace testimony is but one part of a larger witness to the active presence and power of Christ Jesus in our lives. That larger witness is a seamless life of "love, joy, peace, patience, kindness, generosity, faithfulness, gentleness, and self-control"; of keeping the commandments. Murder, stealing, adultery, covetousness, strife, factions, even drunkenness— all these sow the seeds of violence and war (Gal.5:21-23). The first Quakers recognized this key truth and resisted the tendency to make a list of "testimonies," from which one could choose the few one felt comfortable in supporting. They recognized only one witness: that one's entire life had to witness in its actions and words to the presence and power of Christ Jesus.

2. "The Peace Testimony recognizes the basic good of human nature and calls it forth."

While some might quote Scripture out of context, claiming this position rests upon people "seeing our good works and glorifying their Father who is in heaven," such a position is far less religious than philosophical, a humanistic belief that goodness will flower forth if societies with their unjust mores and governments, their violent misguided policies, see our human goodness and quiet their repression. Missed by this position is the logical corollary that the goodness of human nature should beget both good societies and good government. Those who believe in the essential goodness of human nature live lives of denial. They refuse to face the genocidal tendencies in the human heart, the evidence of which has been so appallingly present over the last century.

3. "The Peace Testimony is pacifist."

Still common among twenty-first century Quakers is the tendency to confuse the original Quaker peace testimony with both the pacifist position espoused by members of other "peace churches" and certain early twentieth century political movements. However, a "pacifist" position—"a quiet, passive nonresistance to evil"—was never espoused by original Friends. Their position reflected a strong prophetic tradition: a spiritual tradition that required an active, truthful confrontation of evil, not only with love, but also with God's uncompromising demands for righteousness and justice. This position was not based on a naive belief in the power of love, but rather in an unshakeable faith in God's power.

4. "The 'Modern Quaker Peace Testimony' does not require any foundation in religious tradition or faith, let alone a Christian foundation."

Of all the modern false claims for the peace testimony, this one betrays the sandiest foundation. Such a claim turns the peace testimony into a plant without root, a plant that will quickly wilt in the heat of injustice, violence, and evil—or be eaten away by subtle arguments for violent defense and armed resistance. The lack of a firm foundation betrayed Quakers during the Vietnam era when frustration with the seeming slowness of integration and anger over the continued conflict in Southeast Asia led some to suggest that it was time for violent, rather than nonviolent, resistance. Their optimism concerning nonviolence and the ultimate outcome of the struggle had evaporated.

Moreover, as activist social agendas replaced faith as the foundation for the peace testimony, Friends embraced more and more highly partisan positions, positions that are often part of the problems facing us rather than their solutions. Friends' politics too often drove their practice, and such politics often fostered a blind and brutal self-righteousness little different from ancient militant "God is on our side" arguments.

DISCUSSION QUESTIONS:

1. What evidence can you cite that all Friends do not agree on the Peace Testimony? What form do these disagreements take?
2. What evidence have you found that the Peace Testimony calls forth the basic good of human nature? What evidence have you witnessed that suggests the view that human nature is basically good is in error?
3. Has the Quaker response to evil been one of quiet, passive nonresistance similar to that practice by the Amish? What evidence from Quaker history do you see that might support an alternative characterization that the Quaker response to evil has been one of outspoken, active resistance?
4. Have you seen evidence that the Quaker Peace Testimony not only requires a foundation in faith, but is scattered and lifeless without being founded on Christ Jesus and His commandments? What forms has this evidence taken?

Section 7.E
Friends' Original Peace Witness

Reading: "The [Peace] Declaration of 1660," *The Journal of George Fox* (Nickalls edition), p.398-404.

No document so ably explains the original Quaker peace testimony as the 1660 "Declaration from the harmless innocent people of God, called Quakers, against all sedition, plotters, and fighters in this world...." Unlike our present witness, the peace testimony of the seventeenth century was not based on an unrealistic vision of the world. That declaration addresses a series of questions that might be directed by the world at those who embrace the Christian peace witness, questions that are not explicitly stated in the declaration, but that are nonetheless answered by it.

Below are italicized questions that might be asked, even today, and answers actually given them in the 1660 Declaration[7]:

Why will you not fight?
We can neither kill men, nor swear for nor against them..., because it is contrary to the spirit of Christ, his doctrine, and the practice of his apostles; even contrary to him for whom we suffer all things and endure all things (Fox, p. 401).

Friends' response was simple and direct: Christ Jesus has commanded us not to fight and kill. Of all the reasons for supporting the Peace Testimony, this is its single firm foundation. Even many who support military action and violence under some circumstances—including career military personnel—recognize and honor this as the

---

[7] All references to the 1660 Declaration are from the text published in George Fox's *Journal* (Nickalls edition), pp.398-404.

one true foundation for nonviolent behavior. And they generally respect it and those who truly and sincerely hold to it.

That may be so under the present circumstances, but won't you change your mind when the spirit moves you, when the circumstances change?
We, whom the Lord hath called into the obedience of his truth, have denied wars and fightings, and cannot any more learn them. This is a certain testimony unto all the world of the truth in our hearts in this particular, that as God persuadeth every man's heart to believe, so they may receive it (Fox, p. 400).

But God's commandment not to kill is not absolute, is it?
The spirit of Christ, by which we are guided, is not changeable, so as once to command us from a thing, as evil, and again to move unto it; and we certainly know, and testify to the world, that the spirit of Christ, which leads us into all truth, will never move us to fight and war against any man with outward weapons, neither for the kingdom of Christ nor for the kingdoms of this world (Fox, p. 399-400).

There is a key point here that must not be missed—that God is not changeable. One often hears "continuing revelation" espoused among Friends in support of a number of social agendas that run counter to Scripture and our tradition. "That was then," they say, "but now a new truth has been revealed to us." Such thinking is both erroneous and dangerous to the very peace testimony modern Friends want to embrace. The correct understanding of continuing revelation is: "Yes, more may be revealed, but it will not conflict with prior revelation, because God is not inconsistent, so as to 'command us from a thing as evil and again move on to it.' " If Friends deny this logic, then there is no foundation for the peace testimony, for God would be changeable, sometimes commanding against conflict and, at other moments, moving us to war.

Why will you not fight for your own government and own people?
To this question of allegiances, Friends answered: "We are Christ's people first and citizens of the Kingdom of God foremost." We are not of it [this unrighteous world], but are heirs of a world of which there is no end, a kingdom where no corruptible thing enters.

But are not some wars just, or at least less evil than the alternative of not fighting?
We know that wars and fightings proceed from the lusts of men (James 4:1-3), out of which lusts the Lord hath redeemed us, and so out of the occasion of war. The occasion of which war and war itself (wherein envious men, who are lovers of themselves more than lovers of God, lust, kill, and desire to have men's lives and estates) ariseth from lust. All bloody principles and practices we, as to our own particulars, do utterly deny, with all outward wars, strife, and fighting with outward weapons for any end, or under any pretence whatsoever. And this is our testimony to the whole world (Fox, p. 399).

Why embrace this way [your peace testimony]? *What do you hope to gain?*
Although we have always suffered, and do now more abundantly suffer, yet we know it's for righteousness' sake; 'for all our rejoicing is this, the testimony of our consciences, that in simplicity and godly sincerity, not with fleshly wisdom, but by the grace of God, we have had our conversation in the world' (2 Cor. 1:2), which for us is a witness for the convincing of our enemies (Fox, p.401).

But you will be overwhelmed with the rest of us?!
We earnestly desire and wait, that (by the word of God's power, and its effectual operation in the hearts of men) the kingdoms of this world may become the kingdoms our Lord,

and of his Christ; and that he may rule and reign in men by his spirit and truth; that thereby all people, out of all different judgments and professions, may be brought into love and unity with God, and one with another... (Fox, p. 400).

Will you resist nothing, even the greatest of evils?
To this question, Friends answered they were not "pacifist," not nonresistant to evil. They vigorously opposed evil and injustice, but declared: "Our weapons are spiritual and not carnal, yet mighty through God to the plucking down of the strongholds of Satan, who is the author of wars, fighting, murder, and plots" (Fox, p. 402). In fact, the Declaration, itself, is in part a loving warning for your souls' good, not to wrong the innocent, nor the babes of Christ.

But you have not suffered and you hide behind the protection of others!
Unlike many North American and European Friends today, the first Quakers had suffered the fires of persecution, unjust imprisonment, and martyrdom.

> We have been counted as sheep for the slaughter, persecuted and despised, beaten, stoned, wounded, stocked, whipped, imprisoned, haled out of the synagogues, cast into dungeons and noisome vaults where many have died in bonds, shut up from our friends, denied needful sustenance for many days together, with other the like cruelties (Fox, p. 401).

What if the ultimate happens? You are "driven to earth," killed? Wiped from the face of the earth?!
The cause of all this our sufferings is not for any evil, but for things relating to the worship of our God and in obedience to his requiring of us. For which cause we shall freely give up our bodies a sacrifice, rather than disobey the Lord. For we know, as the Lord hath kept us innocent, so he will plead our cause, when there is none in the earth to plead it. So we, in obedience

unto his Truth, do not love our lives unto death, that we may do his will, and wrong no man in our generation, but seek the good and peace of all men (Fox, p. 401).

It seems you are against everything, our government, our values, us!
Our principle is, and our practices have always been, to seek peace and ensue it and to follow after righteousness and the knowledge of God, seeking the good and welfare and doing that which tends to the peace of all (Fox, p. 399).

Friends often confess, after they've studied the Declaration, "I'm a poor Quaker! I could never embrace this when push came to violence!" That confession is a good starting point for a deeper witness, for early Quakers posited no easy victory, recognizing that indeed they might be "driven to earth," in spite of their goodwill and nonviolence. They recognized that they could not maintain this witness in their own strength, but needed God's power to do so. Their faith was rooted in an understanding of Christ's crucifixion and resurrection: that God's power can be, and is, manifest, even in the face of what seems complete and final death and defeat. If we are truthful, must we not admit our own inability to experience the seeming destruction of all we hold dear? We must admit that we do not have the strength within us to carry through to this end. Jesus, Himself, confessed in the Garden of Gethsemane how daunted He was by the crucifixion that awaited Him. He, Himself, had to seek His Father's power to be obedient and face such a death. A true embrace of the peace testimony must include the real possibility of crucifixion—and the ultimate power of God to turn death into resurrection and victory in ways we cannot see. A true embrace must include our need for God's power to remain faithful to our witness.

DISCUSSION QUESTIONS:

1. At the beginning of this Guide, a framed quote from John H. Curtis relates that early Friends "believed that the Lord had redeemed them from the occasion of war. Christ by His living presence had freed them from war. As a witness or testimony, they were to refrain from it." What is the difference between witnessing for peace because force and violence are wrong, and witnessing for peace because Christ's living presence has freed us from war?
2. Do you think Christ can free you from using force and violence?
3. The peace testimony reflects both the power of evil and the power of God, neither of which translates into secular political rhetoric. Embracing "the real possibility of crucifixion" with the hope of the resurrection does not have a secular analog. How much room does this understanding of the source and conditions for true peace allow for political involvement?
4. What is resonating most within you?

Section 7.F
Simplicity and Plainness

Readings: Matthew 6:33; 1 Corinthians 11:5; 1 Timothy 2:9; Thomas Hamm, *The Quakers in America*, p. 101-108; RULES OF DISCIPLINE OF THE YEARLY MEETING HELD IN PHILADELPHIA (1806) Plainness; NORTH CAROLINA YEARLY MEETING (CONSERVATIVE) DISCIPLINE (1983) Simplicity.

Individual spirituality and group messages. At one time, a Friend was publicly knowable by his or her outward manner of life—language, manners, dress, and home. Simplicity was considered a testimony to the basic importance of God's leading and our submission to Christ. Being a Friend meant living by a specific set of spiritual and practical priorities.

The earliest Friends did not use terms such as "simplicity" or "plainness." They merely thought of themselves as being "obedient." The Scriptures commanded that the Kingdom of God be a Christian's highest priority, which meant that one ought not spend time, money, or energy on unnecessary items or occasions. If the Kingdom of God was one's highest priority, one would, as a consequence, look, speak, and live quite differently than one's neighbors. The Scriptures also had more specific prohibitions, such as a woman wearing jewelry or elaborate hairstyles or praying or prophesying with her head uncovered, or a man wearing long hair or praying or prophesying with his head covered.

By the early eighteenth century, Friends had specific expectations of what their collective witness to the world required in terms of members' styles of life. The names of pagan deities were not to be used for the days and months, but rather the scriptural usage of naming by number. The use of "you" for a singular person was discouraged, as it was associated with the flattery of those in higher social classes. Instead, the more egalitarian "thee" and "thou" were to be used. There were informal, but understood, standards for clothing and lifestyle. But over the next 150 years, this commitment to plainness disappeared, except among the most conservative of Friends.

In Quaker history, simplicity and plainness have in different generations received different emphases. The earliest generation of Friends emphasized simplicity in dress and possessions, without an emphasis on outward, regimented plainness. The earliest Friends tended to frown on such outward regimentation as an overemphasis on the outward, rather than the inward state of one's soul. Later generations up until the twentieth century put more emphasis on plain dress as an outward sign of being a people set apart for God. Quaker simplicity has been defined as shunning possessions and behaviors that obscure the view of true reality and hinder one's responsiveness to God. Although simplicity has become a stated corporate testimony of Friends over the last one hundred years, its practical application has been muddled and lost by lack of emphasis on a useful discipline. Leaving decisions about simplicity to each Friend's individual conscience means essentially there is no longer such a testimony among the great majority of Friends.

How is plainness different? First, plainness is outwardly distinctive. Plainness outwardly indicates membership in a religious fellowship. This invites a specific kind of interaction with others, although it may discourage some.

Second, an individual's plain life manifests the group's message, its convictions as to the practical consequences of seeking the Kingdom of God. It is a group example intended to illuminate not only the spiritual importance of simplicity but the importance of belonging to a spiritually-gathered people. Plainness takes more than one person to bear the group's message.

Third, plainness can sometimes serve as a "hedge," a practical reminder to individuals of their personal commitment to the group's message. Being constantly reminded of one's representative status, one may be less likely to yield to certain temptations.

When individually defined and adopted, simplicity is not as distinctive nor does it clearly manifest a message or membership in a particular group. In that case, simplicity does not act as a "hedge," since individuals can dress simply one day and ostentatiously the next without anyone remarking that any religious significance is attached.

DISCUSSION QUESTIONS:

1. Do you feel you have been called to simplicity? Or to plainness? What factors influence your decisions about simplicity and plainness in "language, manners, dress, and home"?
2. What interactions does plainness encourage? What kinds does it discourage?
3. Do you feel committed to any message for which your group stands? Would you find a hedge (as described above) useful in maintaining your commitment? If so, what would such a hedge be like?
4. One can choose to be simple in one's own way, and in a way that does not make one "stand out" as a Friend. What are the issues raised by being publicly visible as a Friend—or not? Has Western individualism become subversive to developing and maintaining religious community and witness?
5. What is resonating most deeply within you?

Section 7.G
Integrity

Readings: Robert Barclay, *Apology for the True Christian Divinity*, Prop. 15 § 2; RULES OF DISCIPLINE OF THE YEARLY MEETING HELD IN PHILADELPHIA (1806) Gaming and Diversions, Plainness.

Every choice we make in a day either increases or decreases our sensitivity to the Holy Spirit: what we read, buy, and eat; what we wear and where we work; with whom we share our time and what we do in our "spare" time. The care with which we make these decisions is directly related to the care with which we listen for and respond to Christ's Spirit in our life.

Furthermore, many of our choices result in an open witness to other people, even if we do not discuss our decisions with them. For example, the car we drive down the road may become an example for a stranger's choice, as may the clothes we wear. How we spend our money influences other people's income, often directly, as when we purchase locally-grown food, eat at a restaurant, or choose leisure activities for which we pay. The forthrightness, honesty, and kindness of our speech affect family members, friends, and also strangers both directly and as an example. Sarcasm, for instance, asserts the opposite of what is true and, in addition to being simply untruthful, often triggers another untruthful comment or leaves the hearer confused and distanced from the speaker. Sarcasm is especially hurtful for children, undermining their natural sincerity. Friends' traditional refusal to take oaths—that is, to give a special sign that the next statement will be true—is based on Jesus' command to say what you mean, all the time and without subterfuge.

Early Friends were clear about what helped them to be open and obedient to Christ's direction. Living simply, indeed plainly (i.e., living without ostentation, the superfluities of fashion, or unnecessary details); avoiding the distractions and waste of popular entertainment; avoiding unnecessary expenses, while pursuing occupations that left time and energy for spiritual reflection and involvement in the work of God's kingdom: these were all necessary for avoiding being desensitized to God's Spirit by the "vain and corrupt spirit of the world." One cannot live both in the life and time of the world's spirit and in the Eternal Life and Time of God's Spirit.

Likewise in our present-day life, many Friends feel called by God to pursue occupations and manage economic resources in ways that do not conflict with Christ's commands. Good stewardship of the resources God has provided is another aspect of a life of integrity – of being responsive to God's Way and Truth in everything we do. Popular entertainment, while in some ways different from that of earlier generations, continues to present distractions from a life of spiritual integrity.

Early Friends wanted their entire lives to reveal the presence of Christ within them. As they sought to follow Christ's guidance about their outward behavior, they also strove to cultivate and show forth the inward fruits of the Spirit (Galatians 5:22-23). Friends understood that bearing those fruits into the world would mean the seeds of those fruits would be planted to the great increase of God's kingdom.

We can neither receive the Holy Spirit nor bear its fruits when we are full of some other spirit. We cannot be full of love, joy, peace, and patience, when we are opinionated, bitter, selfish, ill tempered, or jealous. These latter are the fruits of being separated from God's will. They are the fruits of a lack of spiritual integrity. By giving them up, we make more space for the Spirit to fill – both within us and within the world outside of us.

DISCUSSION QUESTIONS:

1. What parts of your life reflect integrity between your behavior and your understanding of what God wants? What parts don't?
2. Have you been aware of making major choices in response to God's direction (either immediate direction or as you understand God's intention in general)? Minor choices? Is there a difference with regard to spiritual integrity between major and minor choices? Explain.
3. How can we avoid being spiritually desensitized by the affluence, the entertainment industry, and the consumer culture of today's world?
4. How does making space within us for love, joy, peace, etc., make more space for these fruits of the Spirit in the world outside us?
5. At the very beginning of this Guide, a framed quote from John H. Curtis asserts that "Through the power of Christ [early Friends] were to live lives of honesty, simplicity, and freedom from racial or other forms of prejudice." Could the power of Christ free a whole group of people from deceit, excessive consumption, and prejudice?
6. How might we practice a healthy discipline—one in which we help and encourage one another to live simple, spiritually directed lives—and avoid falling into distracting legalism that leads us away from one another and our Lord's will?
7. What is resonating most deeply within you?

Section 7.H
A Example of Faithful Living — John Woolman

Readings: David Sox, *John Woolman, Quintessential Quaker* (2000); Bill Samuel, Review of David Sox (quakerinfo.com); John Woolman, *Journal and Major Essays* (Phillips Moulton, ed.).

For nearly two hundred and fifty years, many Quakers, especially those who were recorded ministers, kept journals in which they recorded the inward work of God in their souls and the outward manifestations of God's presence and will in their lives. One estimate suggests there are still more than 3000 of these journals extant, many published by past generations, some still available in manuscript in various Quaker historical and digital collections. It is a spiritual literature carefully cultivated, and its publication was taken with great seriousness, for it served as a primer on Quaker spiritual life for following generations. The number of these journals is so large that it rivals the spiritual literature of the Roman Catholic Church on what it means to live in the Spirit and do God's will. One of the best known of these works, *The Journal of John Woolman* (1720-1774), has remained in print for nearly 230 years and is considered a spiritual classic both within and outside the Society of Friends. Woolman was a New Jersey storekeeper, a recorded minister, and a central figure in the early anti-slavery movement. His *Journal* is particularly useful for its record of the challenges he faced in living in God's will in the face of the wars and injustices of his day and in coping with the problems presented by making a living— in Woolman's case, a too successful effort that required spiritual pruning.

Woolman's anti-slavery witness began when, at the age of twenty-three, he refused to write a bill of a sale for a slave. His refusal was based on his clear recognition that slavery was inconsistent with Christianity. Woolman was motivated by both a concern for the slaves—and for the slave owners. He labored with the slave owners gently, but firmly, as equally concerned for their spiritual well-being as he was the spiritual and physical well-being of the slaves. Further, he saw how he himself sometimes inadvertently contributed to the slavery system by utilizing the products it produced, products that made it lucrative and sustained it. He, thus, began wearing only undyed clothes (since slavery were involved in the rich trade of dye production). When Woolman made religious visits to slave owners, he regularly left money for the slaves who waited upon him.

When Woolman's store business flourished, he felt a "stop" in his mind. He was concerned that too much business would distract him from God's call upon his life. Indeed, he gave up retail trade so that he could focus more faithfully on God's call. Woolman believed that buying superfluous items violated the law of love, and the result was to increase misery in the world by requiring unnecessary labor. If we, Woolman insisted, kept our desires strictly upon what was needed, we would live in harmony with God's design and have our needs met with a moderate amount of labor. Woolman understood the satisfaction of our covetous and unnecessary desires is a key cause of much social and spiritual misery.

Woolman wrote that he was "desirous to embrace every opportunity of being inwardly acquainted with the hardship and difficulties of my fellow creatures...." That meant, for example, that he gave up a comfortable cabin on his journey in ministry to England and rather bunked with the sailors in steerage. He also walked in England, rather than use coaches, when he saw the carriage horses were abused and overworked.

DISCUSSION QUESTIONS:

1. Woolman, though he hated slavery, loved both the slave and the slave owner. Why do we find it so easy to condemn our

opponents and demonize them in the name of activism, or politics, or religion?
2. Woolman was exceptional in that he was willing to recognize and confess his guilt, even when he inadvertently erred toward another. Do we recognize our own guilt in participating in the systems we criticize? How and on what basis might we change our ways?
3. Woolman gave up a successful business, believing it interfered with his focus on doing God's will. Do we let the siren call of success and the vague goal of "financial security" divert us from what God would have us do?
4. How do we distinguish between necessity and the superfluous in our affluent society?
5. How might our lives be different if we dispensed with the superfluous? Identify ways.
6. Americans tend to be very judgmental concerning what others own and "get," readily condemning all sorts of activities and purchases. How can we avoid self-righteousness from entering our lives and decisions about how our neighbors live?
7. What is resonating most deeply within you?

Section 7.I
Our Lamb's War Today

Addressing the General Gathering of Conservative Friends in 2006, Jack Smith used early Friends' concept of "the Lamb's War" to call Friends away from materialistic secularism and back to obedience to Christ in all aspects of our lives. After reviewing the meaning of "the Lamb's War" (see in Section B of this chapter), Smith pointed out that "early Friends understood that Jesus Christ was leading them, providing them spiritual weapons, and sustaining them as they submitted to 'the cross of Christ, which is the power of God....' (G. Fox, Epistle 222, 1661)." Jack then continued:

> However, conditions changed dramatically after 1689 when, with the passage of the Acts of Toleration, Friends found permanent relief from the great suffering that they had endured. With the softening of the government's effort to stamp out religious dissent came a softening of the first Friends' stridency and radicalism, ushering in an era now called Quietism. The 1689 London YM advised: "Walk wisely and circumspectly toward all men, in the peaceable Spirit of Jesus Christ, giving no offense nor occasion to those in outward government, nor way to any controversies, heats, or distractions of this world, about kingdoms thereof. But pray for the good of all; and submit all to that Divine power and wisdom which rules over the kingdoms of men" (in Walter Williams, *The Rich Heritage of Quakerism*, p.119). The leadership three years later wrote, "Let all study to be quiet and mind their own business, in God's holy fear..." (Williams, p.120). In his *Let Your Words Be Few*, Richard Bauman observes that the new approach was "not war but diplomacy" (p.145). With the onset of Quietism, Friends abandoned the Lamb's War and no

longer expected to be instruments for the conversion of the entire world to Christ's way.

Ohio Yearly Meeting is the last yearly meeting retaining significant aspects of its Quietist heritage. I believe that conservative Friends are now called to be instruments for God's work under dramatically changing conditions. Is the era of toleration slipping away, to be replaced by challenges that Friends have not known for more than three centuries?

Friends have experienced a slow but steady accommodation to the world. However, important components of Christian unprogrammed faith remain in OYM and are attracting people's attention worldwide. We understand that Jesus Christ is the Word of God, sought and found here with us. We know that the Scriptures were inspired by the Word and have been preserved by God for our use for doctrine, reproof, correction and instruction. We retain our ways of recognizing and nurturing God's gifts among us. We affirm that all of life is under the care of our Lord. Are we, even now, being called to a new work in God's Kingdom? The impact on us individually and as a people could be enormous.

Our attitudes, like those of much of today's world, are influenced by the eighteenth century Enlightenment's conviction that human reason is the road to all truth. This mindset teaches us to question everything and to disdain faith. It fosters a materialistic secularism that functions in many ways like a religion. It views the scientific process as the means to come to knowledge about all reality. As Wilmer Cooper adds, "Basic distinctions between the holy and the profane, the sacred and the secular—even between good and evil—are ignored, if not erased" (*A Living Faith*, p. 29).

Liberal Quakerism asserts that there is "that of God in everyone." Again quoting Wilmer Cooper, "Insofar as 'that of God in everyone' has theological meaning today, its association with Christ has been largely abandoned, whereas for George Fox, this identification was essential. It has also come to mean that God as they understand the deity has been parceled out among all persons so that everyone has a 'piece of God' within, and that it is this that gives worth and dignity to human beings.... Thus, the net effect is a denigration of God and an exaltation of humanity. Somehow, this belies Fox's overwhelming sense that 'the power of the Lord is over all'" (*A Living Faith*, p. 30).

Secular humanism, with its attendant globalization, dominates Western Europe, is gaining in the United States, and expects to permeate the world. Opposed in the US by Evangelical Christians and Roman Catholics, it is being challenged worldwide by an increasingly militant Islam. The gap in this country between rich and poor widens. The media and the entertainment industry—which encourage a materialistic, consuming society—increasingly influence our culture, and even some Christian worship services become a type of superficial entertainment. The physical environment is being plundered and irretrievably changed, with extinctions of many species and loss of essential ecological services. We expect a variety of food year round, sometimes transporting it 6,000 miles. Our federal debt has grown to unimaginable size and depends for financing on people in other parts of the world.

The sustainability of all this must be questioned. What will happen when we reach the breaking point? How far off is that? Will we be prepared if something more cataclysmic than 9/11 occurs?

We need to prepare for a future that may quickly become the present. You know very well that the day of the Lord will come like a thief in the night. While people are saying, "Peace and safety," destruction will come on them suddenly, as labor pains on a pregnant woman, and they will not escape. But you, brothers, are not in darkness so that this day should surprise you like a thief. You are all sons of the light and sons of the day. We do not belong to the night or to the darkness. So then, let us not be like others, who are asleep, but let us be alert and self-controlled (1 Thess. 5:2-6). What do we need to do to prepare ourselves? Jesus spoke about preparation in the parable of the wise and foolish virgins (Matt 25: 1-13). Our best preparation is learning faithful trust, attention, and obedience to God through Christ.

We Westerners enjoy and now expect many blessings: lights that turn on with the flick of a switch, safe water that pours from our faucets, dependable transportation, abundant consumer goods, and personal safety as we walk, travel, work, and worship. There are many more. Do we assume that these blessings will continue? Can they continue? Do we require these blessings in order to feel blessed? Could we feel blessed under adversity?

Early Friends lived under adversity. They were beaten, imprisoned, and even killed. They were hailed before judges and had their goods taken. They were social outcasts, yet they thrived and the Friends' movement grew and flourished. They saw themselves in the midst of the Lamb's War, that epic struggle between the Lamb Jesus Christ and Satan with his forces of evil.

In this struggle, there is no place for lukewarmness. In the Lamb's War, Christians are called to follow Christ into battle as citizens of His kingdom, prepared and equipped by Him. Paul described that equipment: Therefore put on the full armor of God, so that when the day of evil comes, you may be able to stand your ground, and after you have done everything, to stand. Stand firm then, with the belt of truth buckled around your waist, with the breastplate of righteousness in place, and with your feet fitted with the readiness that comes from the gospel of peace. In addition to all this, take up the shield of faith, with which you can extinguish all the flaming arrows of the evil one. Take the helmet of salvation and the sword of the Spirit, which is the word of God (Ephesians 6:13-17).

The Lamb's War seems foolish to the world, for following Christ into that battle requires following the way of the cross. Jesus yielded Himself to His Father's will and suffered, allowing the forces of evil to destroy His life. In His resurrection, which we experience through His continuing presence among us, we find God's ultimate victory over evil. As Christians, we must follow Christ—in truth, righteousness, peace, and faith—through whatever outward circumstances He leads us. We must be prepared both to suffer and to know Christ's joy.

DISCUSSION QUESTIONS:

1. At the very beginning of this Guide, a framed quote from John H. Curtis proclaims that the people of God who follow Christ "die, yet they have eternal life. They suffer, yet they rejoice. They are weak and frail, yet they are made more than conquerors." Have you ever suffered, yet rejoiced, or felt weak and yet overcome difficulties through strength that came from beyond you? What was your experience?

2. Can one generation convey its faith to its children? Or must the work of the Holy Spirit begin again with each new generation, in spite of our own best efforts to preserve and transmit our faith and practice?
3. What is your understanding of the degree of sustainability of our present Western culture? What do you, personally, feel called to do to maintain the cultural and spiritual blessings you enjoy? For whom do you hope to be able to maintain them? What do you think other people should do? Friends should do corporately?
4. Do we require those blessings to feel blessed? Have you ever felt blessed in adversity? What spiritual preparation is likely to be of help for dealing with a reduction of cultural and economic blessings? What, if any, of that preparation can we do corporately as a body of Friends together?
5. What is resonating most deeply within you?

APPENDICES

Appendix 1: Readings on Eldership
Appendix 2: A Glossary to Quaker Terminology
Appendix 3: Modern Quakerism, A Fragmented Society:
Historic Separations among Friends
Appendix 4: A Bibliography for Further Reading

Appendix 1: Eldering and Oversight Readings

We deemed it cost prohibitive and beyond our means to generate an appendix that would have included all the readings we recommend in the "Reading" suggestions at the opening of the various sections of this Guide. However, we have chosen to include the following material on Eldering and Oversight, because so much misinformation surrounds them today and so little accurate understanding and material exist on the true spiritual nature of these important spiritual gifts and offices among Quakers.

A Plea for Strong Eldership
From Seth Hinshaw's blog piece
from 3/28/2010 in *Chronicler's Minutiae*
at http://chronicler-3.blogspot.com

"Then fourteen years after, I went up again to Jerusalem with Barnabas, and took Titus with me also. And I went up by revelation, and communicated unto them that gospel which I preach among the Gentiles, but privately to them which were of reputation, lest by any means I should run, or had run, in vain" Galatians 2:1-2. In this passage, the apostle makes a remarkable statement—after a time of ministry, he went to visit those "of reputation" to find out if he had run in vain. If such a visit was needed by Paul, how can any of us believe that we need any less?

In the Society of Friends, people named Elders provide feedback to ministers, guiding them around the pitfalls and nurturing them with the spiritual guidance wherein they appear lacking. Most groups of Friends scaled back the duties of Elders in the late nineteenth century and throughout the twentieth century because of a reticence that anyone else should "judge" the leadings of a minister. Now, in the early twenty-first century, the position is beginning to emerge again in various places. In some Midwestern FGC yearly meetings, the role of Elder is played by people serving on what are called "anchoring committees." Philadelphia Yearly Meeting has recently started appointing Elders to serve as something of "silent observers" during business meetings, who attempt to foster the sense of worship during the deliberations. Although these varied interpretations of the office may not be consistent in their intent, some general principles appear to hold among all groups of Friends.

Ministers need Elders. This statement is so obvious that it seems pointless to mention. No matter how much a minister attempts to be true to the Guide in speaking, mistakes are made. The problem is this: often, when someone speaks under a false leading during worship, there is a possibility that a hearer will be turned away—not from the speaker—but instead from Christ Jesus. Such an event is a major problem, particularly if it continues. One role of the Elder is to look out for anything that takes away from a person's ministry, emphasizing the strengths and guiding the minister away from shortcomings. Elders are not the enemies of ministers—in fact, Elders work to help ministers grow in their gift and improve their ability to follow the guidance of the Light of Christ even better.

The two therefore have a **joint exercise of gifts.** Meetings of ministers and elders were instituted over 300 years ago. Of course, in the seventeenth century, Friends understood there to be more of an overlap between the two offices, and Friends were not being specifically named to either office until the early eighteenth century. The overseers have participated in these meetings [in OYM] since 1958. When Friends with diverse gifts gather to discuss the things of the Spirit, individual gifts are sharpened as Friends grow in their yearning to help each part of the body to function at its best. Those in all three stations need to be good listeners, both to the Lord and to each other. To use an analogy from the world, they are all part of the same team, and not in competition with each other.

No. It is a great irony that one of the most powerful words in the English language is also one of the shortest. The word "no" is a word that those who speak on the Lord's behalf need to hear sometimes. Most Elders are able to work around a direct "no" by saying something like "I wouldn't do that now," but the fact stands that ministers need to know when they are straying from the path. The relationship between a minister and an Elder must be well-nurtured and strong in order that the caution may be received in the right spirit. Ministers need to hear "What thee is doing is undermining thy ministry" if the Lord has shown that to an Elder. As someone who hardly ever hears "no," I can say without hesitation that when I hear it, I take notice.

Last year, a woman was telling a story in a conversation among four Friends (including me). As part of the conversation, the woman said that if God told someone to do something but the Elders counseled against it, the person should go ahead and do it anyway. This really bothered me. To begin with, if the Lord gave a person direction, that person should be able to convey a sense of the gravity of the leading to the Elders. If rightly appointed Elders believe it not to be "of the Lord," I told her that I would definitely hesitate to do the thing. There is safety in the multitude of counselors, because whether we like it or not, each of us occasionally finds it difficult to discern between ego and God. Last, if it is a true leading, the Lord would grant the Elders strength to see His hand in the matter.

* * * * *

Insights into the Practice of Eldering in Ohio Yearly Meeting
Minutes from a consideration of eldering during the session of Ohio Yearly Meeting for Ministry and Oversight, 8-9-2011

There is a natural gravitation to elders by people who are in need of eldering, including some who do not know why they are troubled. An elder can be seen as a Friend who gives trustworthy advice about our life following Christ. Not availing oneself of an elder's counsel is like ignoring advice from a qualified teacher in one's work place.

We find that elders have wisdom and discernment given them by God. Elders can listen well to people who come for advice or for clarification of some spiritual situation they find troubling. They often listen to their own spiritual leadings and are able to share helpfully with others how we can listen and respond to God. Elders need to be tender and sensitive in the timing and strength of their counsel that tender spiritual buds not be bruised.

Some ministers among us today have noted that they may become overconfident in their gift or have difficulty dividing their own concerns from the message that comes from God. Elders have assisted them in not straying from what God gives them. Likewise, elders help hold ministers accountable and responsive to the meeting. One minister remembers an elder telling her when she was much younger, "I can feel the Spirit in thy spoken ministry, but I cannot hear thee. Speak up." Today, that minister's speaking is clearly audible throughout the room. In addition, an elder can be a conduit for a concern an individual member has, without requiring that Friend to go directly to the minister.

Many of us sense that there is a cross in doing the Lord's work, as well as a vibrant joy. We need to feel the weight of that cross, and we need one another to help bear it. It is important for meetings at every organizational level to become aware of budding spiritual gifts and to encourage their growth. Then our meetings will continue to have leadership with that subtle touch which reminds us of the true and fundamental leadership of our Lord, Christ Jesus.

Appendix 2: A Brief Glossary to Quaker Terminology

The language of faith must be learned. It is rarely translatable into secular or scientific terminology and never with much accuracy. The language of faith is, in part, the language of Scriptures and, in part, the language souls have developed to describe and express their experience of God and His direction. The Quakers, early in their history in the seventeenth and eighteenth centuries, developed a rich faith language in which to express themselves. To help our readers become familiar with this language and to enter upon a deeper experience of traditional Quaker Christianity, we offer the following glossary.

ADVICES. The collected wisdom and experience of Friends written and used as reminder of the faith and practices held to be essential to the life and witness of Friends.

AFFIRMATION. A legal declaration made by one who refuses to swear an oath (a declaration that one will tell the truth in a particular matter, while recognizing it is the way of the world to lie). The affirmation is a declaration that one tells the truth at all times.

APPRECIATE. To approve of, and be thankful for; often of a person's action.

AS ABLE. When (a person is) ready or feeling led by God.

AS WAY OPENS. When relevant circumstances are appropriate and obstacles are gone.

BIRTHRIGHT MEMBER. One who was born of Quaker parents and recorded at birth on a monthly meeting's membership rolls, as opposed to a convinced Friend (see below).

BREAKING MEETING. Term used for the closing of meeting for worship when a designated Friend discerns the conclusion of worship and signals other Friends, usually by shaking hands with the person next to him or her.

CENTERED. Being consciously directed towards the Presence of Christ, often used to describe an experience during meeting for worship.

CLEARNESS. A condition of being clear on what God's will is on a particular matter. Clearness may be experienced by individuals or by entire meetings.

CLEARNESS COMMITTEE. A group of Friends appointed or selected to assist a person or the meeting to clarify a decision or concern.

CLERK. A member who presides at business meetings of Friends. The clerk's work is to collect items of business for the meeting's agenda, arrange them in appropriate order, and record the sense of the meeting with respect to decisions made or actions taken. The clerk is neither a clergy person nor the spiritual leader of the meeting (Jesus Christ is), and never should be viewed as "the minister," a "pastor," or the leader of the meeting. The clerk is simply a servant of the meeting.

CONCERN. A deep and spiritual interest held by either an individual or a meeting. An urgent interest, implicitly God-given; does not imply worry. As a noun: "I have a concern for our youth"; or, as a verb, "I am concerned that we not act hastily." "Concern" is less a human assertion of divine action than a "leading."

CONTINUING REVELATION. The belief that Christ continues to speak directly to us, revealing to us His Will in specific matters. Since God is not a God of confusion or contradiction, such revelations confirm and are in line with prior revelations. "New" revelations do not cancel out and replace prior revelations.

CONVINCED FRIEND. A person who becomes a Friend as a result of being "convicted" by the Light as to his or her sinful spiritual state and who is drawn by the Spirit to live in obedience to God's will and in unity with Friends' principles and witness. ("Convinced" is an archaic form of "convicted.")

CORPORATE. Referring to a body of Friends. For example, the corporate witness of a meeting.

CONSERVATIVE FRIENDS. Those Friends who seek to conserve what they believe is essential in Friends' traditions. At the very least, this is usually considered to be unprogrammed worship and a Christian faith. In some cases, it may also include certain aspects of traditional Friends' lifestyles, such as plainness.

COVERED MEETING. A meeting during which Friends share an exceptional sense of the Lord's Presence, often in a deep and shared stillness.

ELDERING. A respected Friend's or group of Friends' encouraging or admonishing another Friend as to some specific matter of concern.

ELDERS. Those with a special gift and burden for encouraging and admonishing other Friends, especially as to vocal ministry during worship and to advise and counsel concerning spiritual development or spiritual problems. Elders may be recognized and recorded by their meeting.

EVANGELICAL FRIENDS. Those Friends whose Christian understanding has been substantially influenced by evangelical faith and practice outside of the Society of Friends. Some evangelical

Friends emphasize a single-conversion experience. Some emphasize holiness. Some are more liberal. Some also emphasize Quaker distinctives, such as the Quaker testimonies. Evangelical Friends' meetings tend to employ professional pastors and use programmed worship, with little or nominal waiting worship.

EXERCISE. A spiritual struggle that can attend a meeting or an individual working toward clearness on what the will of God is in a particular matter. An intense spiritual labor (noun), often with "considerable," like "After considerable exercise, we reached unity."

EXERCISED. Deeply troubled spiritually (usually passive verb form): "I was exercised by the boys' war games."

FACING BENCHES. The benches or seats in the front of the meeting room, facing the body of the meeting, on which recorded ministers and recorded elders or, in their absence, those charged with breaking meeting usually sit.

GATHERED MEETING. A meeting during which Friends share an exceptional sense of the Lord's activity gathering Friends into a deep sense of unity, often through united themes of vocal ministry.

GOOD ORDER. The procedures traditionally used by Friends to facilitate meetings.

GOSPEL ORDER. The order brought by obedience to Christ.

HOLD IN THE LIGHT. To pray that Christ's Light be known to certain persons in an exceptional way, especially a comforting way.

INWARD LIGHT. This refers to the power and inspiration of Christ coming inwardly to us to show us our motivations and true selves, correct us, guide us, and lead us, and give us strength to act on this guidance. It thus brings us into unity with the spirit of God.

The "Inward Light" is also called the "Light Within," the "Christ Within," the "Light of Christ," the "Holy Spirit," and "The Seed."

LEADING. An inward conviction that Christ is directing one to take a specific action.

LIBERAL FRIENDS. Those Friends who insist on the spiritual freedom of individual Friends and who seek to articulate their religious understandings in a manner consistent with the most contemporary movements in the natural and social sciences, the arts, and other aspects of secular culture. Liberal Friends were historically influenced by the Unitarian/Universalist religious movement of the first half of the nineteenth century. The Quaker manifestation of that influence is termed Hicksism and is found also among twentieth century "modernist" Gurneyites. Theologically, Liberal Friends tend to question the usefulness of the Scriptures and the divinity of Jesus.

MEETING. In contemporary usage, this usually refers to the local congregation that meets weekly for worship and monthly for business. A "quarterly meeting" is comprised of representatives of related monthly meetings meeting quarterly for business, while the "yearly meeting" is the annual meeting of members and representatives from related monthly and quarterly meetings.

MINDING THE LIGHT. An exhortation to be consciously centered on the Light of Christ and concerned with doing His will, especially during a trying time.

MINUTE. A statement of the sense of the meeting, its unity in Christ, with respect to a specific item considered in a meeting for business.

MOVED TO SPEAK. Being moved by the Holy Spirit to speak usually during a meeting for worship.

NEAR. Spiritually close and intimate, not "close" meaning "almost." "There was near unity" means "We were drawn tightly together."

OPENING. Moment of revelation, enlightenment, or inspiration from Christ, often unexpected.

OVERSEERS. Those Friends with a special charge by the meeting to exercise pastoral care in the meeting, especially with respect to practical needs. (Overseers would be called "deacons" in some other denominations.)

PLAIN DRESS. Simple, but distinctive, dress intended to witness Friends' convictions to others and to remind the wearer of the same. Some Friends are called to plain dress, others to simple dress. There is no outward regimentation of dress as there is among the Amish and some Mennonite sects.

PLAIN SPEECH. The "thee," "thy," and "thine" used by Friends, especially up to the early twentieth century. In the 1600s, a wealthy person or member of the nobility was addressed by the plural pronoun "you" while inferiors or children were addressed by the singular pronoun "thou." Friends and many others refused to recognize such distinctions. Because the days and months were named for non-Christian gods, goddesses, and emperors, Friends preferred to use "first-day," "second-day," "First Month," "Second Month," etc. The term "plain speech" also refers to forthright and divinely-led speech.

PROGRAMMED MEETING. A meeting for worship with a predetermined formatting of speaking, silence, singing, or other activities. Programmed meetings with substantial periods of silent waiting are often called "semi- programmed."

PROCEED AS WAY OPENS. To await further divine guidance with respect to a specific issue, especially as the circumstances surrounding the issue continue to develop.

PURPOSING. Intending.

QUERIES. Specific written questions used as an opportunity for individuals and meetings to examine themselves (and be examined) with respect to the faith and practices held to be essential to the life and witness of Friends.

SEASONING. A process to ensure that decisions are truly grounded in God's will.

SENSE OF THE MEETING. A perception of Truth that emerges from the corporate business process as Friends seek Christ's will with respect to a specific decision. If the clerk feels that a decision has been reached, he or she states the sense of the meeting as a minute for the meeting's approval. No vote is taken. The clerk must discern if unity is present and produce a minute reflecting that unity.

SPEAK TO ONE'S CONDITION. The experience of receiving a message directly from God, or through another person, that touches one at the deepest level or helps one solve a problem or make a right decision.

STANDING ASIDE. The withdrawal of opposition by a member not able to unite with a proposed minute, thus freeing the meeting to proceed. The member does not feel a spiritual stop to the action nor a sense that the action before the meeting goes against God's will.

STANDING IN THE WAY. The declaration of a member unable to unite with a proposed minute. Requires the item of business to be laid aside until such time as the meeting finds spiritual unity through waiting upon Christ Jesus.

A STOP, or A STOP IN THE MIND. An expression used by Friends to indicate a deeply-felt spiritual inability to proceed with a course of action, even though the Friend may not be able to articulate fully what is specifically objectionable about the action.

UNIVERSALIST FRIENDS. Those Friends who consider the essence of Quakerism to transcend Christianity and be consistent with spiritual seekers of any or no religious orientation. Universalist Friends embrace "hyphenated Quakerism," such as Buddhist-Quakerism, Christocentric Quakerism, Non-Theistic Quakerism, and Jewish Quakerism.

UNITY. A shared perception in a business meeting that a conclusion represents the Friends' best understanding of God's will on a specific issue.

UNPROGRAMMED MEETING. A meeting for worship sometimes erroneously referred to as a "silent meeting." The essence is that Friends await the immediate guidance of Christ as to when and what ought be spoken. More traditional terms are "waiting worship," "expectant worship," or "silence before the Lord."

USEFUL. The choice in keeping with God's will (example of understatement).

VISITATION. Intentional visiting among Friends for any specific purpose.

WAIT UPON THE LORD. Actively to seek and attend to God's will in expectant, quiet worship.

WEIGHTY FRIEND. A Friend whom others informally recognize as having special experience and being gifted with spiritual wisdom.

WITNESS. Used as a noun or a verb; testifying to or showing evidence of religious beliefs and convictions, or the act of doing so, as in "the witness of our lives."

WORLDLY. Manifesting the non-Christian spirit and values or lack of them opposed to God's will and the teaching of Jesus Christ.

Appendix 3: Modern Quakerism, A Fragmented Society

Historic Separations among Friends

*"You need a map, a lexicon,
and a code book to tell who's who among these Quakers today."*
-from an traveler among Twenty-First Century Quakers

Readings: Lewis Benson, *A Universal Quaker Faith* (aka as *Catholic Quakerism*); Thomas Hamm, *The Quakers in America*, Ch. 3.

The Orthodox-Hicksite Separations: Toward the end of the eighteenth century, some Friends began to be significantly influenced by broader movements, such as individualism, liberal Protestant theology, deism, and, some while later, spiritualism. Two separations took place in this context, one in Ireland over the role of the Scriptures, and one in New England where some Friends—the "New Lights"—denied the divinity of Jesus and emphasized their immediate inspiration to reject traditional practices (and, for example, take-up wearing swords). News of these separations caused great concern among many American Friends who grew concerned about the spiritual decline among Friends and who sought to uphold the substance of Friends faith.

These Friends were the Orthodox Friends, who were diverse in many respects—some more open than others to cooperating with evangelicals, for example—but who were united in certain beliefs:

> With some slight differences of opinion they held to the simple statements of the Gospels concerning the miraculous birth of Jesus Christ and to His essential oneness with the Father and with the Holy Spirit, though they preferred not to use the word Trinity, as being non-

scriptural. While not calling the Bible the "Word of God," which they reserved for Christ, they firmly believed in its inspiration. While the Spirit was primary, they maintained that the Scriptures bore testimony to the Spirit and the Spirit to the Scriptures, so that to be completely furnished both are needed. They held that the sacrifice of Jesus Christ on the cross was necessary for the sins of the whole world, and that through this sacrifice the gift of the Spirit is given to every man that cometh into the world. They believed that the light of Christ shone into the hearts of all, and that everyone would be judged according to the light given to him (Allen C. and Richard H. Thomas, *The History of the Friends in America*, 1919).

The Orthodox Friends soon began focusing their objections on a popular minister from New York Yearly Meeting who they believed embodied the influences of the secular world they feared would undermine the Society. His name was Elias Hicks. They believed that he denied the divinity of Jesus Christ and His sacrificial death, or, at the least, that he understood them in a way different from what Friends had historically. As the Orthodox Friends moved to censure Hicks, he gained a considerable number of supporters. Most of these supporters were not necessarily sympathetic to Hicks' views, as such, but rather supported his individual freedom of religion. The Orthodox, however, did not consider Hicks as an individual but rather as a recorded minister of New York Yearly Meeting, which was a specific and special office. In the role of a recorded minister, Hicks had considerable influence, but he was also subject to the elders' oversight.

Thus, the resulting tensions involved concern over not only faith but also practice—how much power should the elders have to regulate the ministers?

The conflict grew until 1827 and 1828, when it split five American yearly meetings: Philadelphia, New York, Baltimore,

Indiana, and Ohio. Numerically, about 60 percent of Friends were Orthodox, and about 40 percent were Hicksites. The numbers in any given yearly meeting varied, of course. The historical result was two groups of yearly meetings, and the permanent disintegration of the Society of Friends. The united Society of Friends that had ended the eighteenth century was now split into two groups, each claiming to be the one true Society.

Orthodox Schisms. After the Hicksite-Orthodox separation, the Orthodox Friends themselves began to divide into different groups.[8] Generally, the divisions among Orthodox Friends were between a minority who wanted to maintain traditional Quaker theology (as expressed in Barclay's *Apology*) and traditional Quaker lifestyle and the Orthodox Friends who sought a greater consistency with the theology and lifestyles of evangelical Protestants. These divisions began in the 1840s and have lasted into the twenty-first century.

The initial divisions coalesced around the ministry of Joseph John Gurney. He was a prominent English Friend who toured American meetings with great success. Gurney believed that early Friends had erred on certain theological issues. He distinguished between "justification" and "sanctification," which early Friends insisted were one process of reconciliation with God. While he believed that Friends should retain their commitments to their testimonies such as waiting worship, the ministry of women, and peace, he encouraged cooperation with evangelical Protestants on

---

[8] During the nineteenth century, separations and schisms were in no way unique to Quakers. They seemed to be a characteristic of the age. As the century progressed, schisms occurred between large numbers of Protestants, especially in New England where Unitarianism challenged the Trinitarian views of theologically orthodox Christians. The strife over slavery, culminating in the Civil War, led not only the separations between Northern Protestants and their Southern Brethren, but even between white congregations and African-American congregations (like the African Methodist Episcopal Church).

common causes. Evangelicals, at this time, were noted especially for their social work with the poor and in seeking social reforms.

The Friend whose name came to symbolize conservative opposition to "Gurneyism" was John Wilbur. Conservatives characterized Gurney as a "restless spirit," and believed that his distinction between justification and sanctification, while maintaining the role of faith in salvation, deemphasized, perhaps disregarded, the need of that faith to produce works. The leaders of Wilbur's Yearly Meeting—New England—were "Gurneyites" who disowned Wilbur for his criticisms of Gurney. About 10 percent of the Friends in New England Yearly Meeting formed a conservative Yearly Meeting in response, and the division—between "Conservatives" and "Gurneyites"—through other yearly meetings, with the Gurneyites in the majority in most yearly meetings. The pace and extent of the changes varied from place to place. By 1900, some Gurneyites embraced evangelical theology and cooperation with other Christians but continued with unprogrammed worship and emphasis on the traditional Quaker testimonies. However, most Gurneyites were moving to embrace programmed meetings with paid pastors. Though a minority of Gurneyites pled for a return to traditional Quaker faith and practice, this minority was outnumbered about 8:1.

Over the next fifty years, Gurneyite Quakerism underwent substantial changes of the sort the Conservatives predicted. The enthusiasm to cooperate with evangelical Protestants and the Gurneyite understanding of justification by faith at the expense of works that were the proof of that salvation opened Gurneyite Friends to mainstream Protestant practices. Several trends among Gurneyites were taken to their logical conclusion. First was the trend to abolish the distinctive lifestyle of Friends. Second was the use of programmed meetings, which were initially justified as "teaching" meetings to attract new converts to Quakerism but soon became interdenominational "revival" meetings in many places. Third was the use of professional pastors, who were initially hired in order to minister to the new converts recruited through the revival meetings. Thus, by 1875, a Methodist minister to a Gurneyite yearly meeting reported he felt as at home as he would at a Methodist meeting.

The Current Situation Among Friends

The time-honored term *Quaker* once meant something very clear. It denoted a radical faithfulness to Christ Jesus who Friends experienced as present and powerful, both in their lives and in the world. It denoted a polity, a faith, an obedience to the Lord in the way life was to be lived keeping His commandments (not a *lifestyle*, as that fashionable but unreal and meaningless term implies). It denoted a system of faith and practice in which everything was structured to maximize the presence, power, and direction of Christ Jesus in the lives of His followers.

At least four current divisions of Friends today claim the name of Quaker to varying degrees, degrees so diverse as to suggest that most have largely divorced themselves from the original Quaker revelation, faith, doctrine, and practices.

LIBERALISM. Liberalism among Friends can be traced to the Hicksite defense of spiritual individualism. The spiritual freedom of individual Friends is perhaps the most important principle of liberal Quakerism. Liberalism among Friends, however, has a second source, which is found in Gurneyite Quakerism. One of the groups of Gurneyite Friends who objected to the "holiness" and "revivalist" influences on Gurneyites became a progressive, liberal influence in Quakerism. Their liberalism sought to make Quakerism consistent with the trends in science, education, arts, and politics. Liberalism among Friends today is found among both unprogrammed meetings and pastoral meetings. It has been substantially influenced by mainstream liberal theology, politics, and culture. Pastoral liberal Friends tend to be affiliated with Friends United Meeting, while unprogrammed liberal Friends tend to be affiliated with Friends General Conference or one of the "independent" western yearly meetings (e.g., Pacific Yearly Meeting).

UNIVERSALISM AND THE RISE OF THE HYPHENATED QUAKER. Rufus Jones was a liberal Gurneyite Friend who claimed that the early Quakers were mystics who had only nominal convictions about Jesus of Nazareth. Although Jones identified as a Christian, his writings paved the way for the growth of universalism among Friends. Quaker universalism describes Quakerism as a mystical spirituality that transcends Christianity and other religions. For the universalist, Quakerism is a method that can be shared by spiritual seekers of all the world's religions and those who claim no religion. Among universalist Quakers are those who self-describe as Buddhist-Quaker, Pagan-Quaker, Jewish-Quaker, Wiccan-Quaker, and Non-Theist-Quaker. Those universalist Quakers who identify themselves as Christians usually prefer the term "Christocentric Quaker." Universalist Quakerism, in this sense, is almost entirely confined to unprogrammed meetings affiliated with Friends General Conference or one of the "independent" western yearly meetings (e.g., Intermountain Yearly Meeting).

EVANGELICALISM. While some pastoral meetings are liberal Christian congregations with many similarities to mainline liberal denominations, most pastoral meetings are evangelical. Some of these Friends identify more with the wider evangelical movement than with Quakerism, though other evangelical Friends value their Quaker identity at least as much as their evangelical one. Some evangelical Friends also identify with the Wesleyan Holiness movement or the

Fundamentalist movement. Most evangelical congregations are affiliated with Evangelical Friends International, while many are affiliated with Friends United Meeting.

CONSERVATIVE QUAKERISM. Conservative Friends believe themselves to have preserved the essence of historic Quakerism, understood, at a minimum, to be unprogrammed worship and a Christian identity. However, conservative Friends are by no means uninfluenced by the larger movements among Friends. Perhaps conservative Friends might be best understood as the group least influenced by the other movements—but influenced nonetheless. Thus, there are conservative versions of liberal, universalist, and evangelical Friends, but they tend to be more moderate than their counterparts in other Quaker branches. The result is considerable diversity among "conservative" Friends. Those who continue to find the witness of early Friends the most consistent with their own experiences are, of course, the most conservative of the conservatives, but, as has been true since the first Orthodox divisions, the least in number. There are three conservative yearly meetings, none of which is affiliated with a larger body of Friends, though the term "conservative" is also claimed by individual Friends in other yearly meetings.

Appendix 4: A Bibliography for Further Reading

General Reading

Anonymous. *The Concurrence and Unanimity of the People Called Quakers as Evidenced by Some of Their Sermons,* Edited with introductions by Patrick J. Burns and T.H.S. Wallace. Camp Hill, PA: Foundation Publications, 2010.

Barclay's Apology in Modern English. Edited by Dean Freiday. 1967.

Barclay, Robert. *An Apology for the True Christian Divinity.* Farmington, ME: Quaker Heritage Press. First published in 1678.

Bates, Elisha. *Doctrines of Friends.* 1824.

Berk, Arthur. *George Fox and the Bible.* Camp Hill, PA: Foundation Publications.

Fell, Margaret. *A Sincere and Constant Love: An Introduction to the Works of Margaret Fell.* Richmond, IN: Friends United Press, 1992, 2nd edition in 2009.

Fell, Margaret. *Undaunted Zeal: The Letters of Margaret Fell.* Edited and introduce by Elsa F. Glines, Richmond, IN: Friends United Press, 2003.

Fox, George. *The Journal of George Fox.* Edited by John L. Nickalls. London: Religious Society of Friends, 1975.

Fox, George. *The Works of George Fox.* 8 volumes. 1831 edition, State College, PA: New Foundation Publication, 1990.

Jones, T. Canby. *George Fox's Attitude toward War.* Richmond, IN: Friends United Press, 1972.

Penington, Isaac. *The Works of Isacc Penington: A Minister of the Gospel in the Society of Friends, Including His Collected Letters.* 4 volumes. Glenside, PA: Quaker Heritage Press, 1995.

Penn, William. *No Cross, No Crown: A Discourse Showing the Nature and Discipline of the Holy Cross of Christ, and that the Denial of Self and Daily Bearing of Christ's Cross is the Alone Way to the Rest and Kingdom of God.* York, England: The Ebor Press, 1981.

Skidmore, Gil. *Strength in Weakness: Writings by Eighteenth Century Quaker Women.* Walnut Creek, CA: AltaMira Press, 2003.

Stirredge, Elizabeth. *Strength in Weakness Manifest: Elizabeth Stirredge, 1634-1706, with an Introduction and Notes by T.H.S. Wallace.* Camp Hill, PA: Foundation Publications, 2011.

Wilbur, John. *Letters to a Friend, on Some of the Primitive Doctrines of Christianity.* Philadelphia, PA: The Tract Association of Friends, 1832 (TAF edition 1995).

Ohio Yearly Meeting Histories

A Brief History of Ohio Yearly Meeting of the Religious Society of Friends (Conservative). Compiled by Charles P. Morlan. Published at the direction of The Representative Meeting, Barnesville, Ohio: 1959.

Anonymous. *A Short History of Conservative Friends.* Snowcamp, [n.d.]. www.snowcamp.org/shocf/shocframe.html

Morse, Kenneth S. P. *A History of Conservative Friends, Consisting of a History of Ohio Yearly Meeting, Somerset Monthly Meeting (Ohio), and other Conservative Bodies in America.* Barnesville, Ohio: 1962.

Taber, William P., Jr. *The Eye of Faith: A History of Ohio Yearly Meeting, Conservative.* Barnesville, OH. Representative Meeting of Ohio Yearly Meeting, Religious Society of Friends, 1985.

A Selection of Journals and Writings by Ohio Yearly Meeting Friends

Nineteenth Century

Branson, Ann. *Journal of Ann Branson, a Minister of the Gospel in the Society of Friends.* Philadelphia, PA: W.H. Pile's Sons, Printers, 1892.

Edgerton, Joseph. *Some Account of the Life and Religious Services of Joseph Edgerton, a Minister of the Gospel with Extracts from His Correspondence.* Philadelphia, PA: William H. Pile, Printer, 1885.

Maule, Joshua. *Transactions and Changes in the Society of Friends, and Incidents in the Life and Experience of Joshua Maule. With a Sketch of the Original Doctrine and Discipline of Friends. Also a Brief Account of the Travels and Work in the Ministry of Hannah Hull, of Ohio.* J. B. Lippincott, 1886.

Ratcliff, Mildred. *Memoranda and Correspondence of Mildred Ratcliff.* Ohio Yearly Meeting, 1890.

Twentieth Century

Carl Patterson. *A Biography and Extracts of Writings.* Ohio Yearly Meeting, 1949.

Cooper, Cyrus. *Memorial to Cyrus Cooper and Bertha A. Cooper.* Moorestown, NJ: Samuel Cooper, 1948.

Cooper Wilmer. *The Testimony of Integrity in the Society of Friends.* Wallingford, PA: Pendle Hill Pamphlet #296.

Taber, Frances Irene. *Finding the Taproot of Simplicity.* Wallingford, PA: Pendle Hill Pamphlet #400.

Digital Resources

DQC: The Digital Quaker Collection. ESR.Earlham.edu/dqc

Earlham School of Religion's digital collection of 500 individual works from 17th and 18th Quakers.

Made in the USA
Middletown, DE
05 March 2017